betrayed *not* BROKEN

betrayed
not BROKEN

From Discovery to

Decision Making

———

Your Journey

Through Infidelity

LAUREL WIERS

New York

betrayed ⁓not⁓ BROKEN
From Discovery to Decision Making; Your Journey Through Infidelity

Published in New York, New York, by Morgan James Publishing. Morgan James and The Entrepreneurial Publisher are trademarks of Morgan James, LLC. www.MorganJamesPublishing.com

The Morgan James Speakers Group can bring authors to your live event. For more information or to book an event visit The Morgan James Speakers Group at www.TheMorganJamesSpeakersGroup.com.

ISBN 978-1-63047-218-4 paperback
ISBN 978-1-63047-219-1 eBook
ISBN 978-1-63047-220-7 hardcover
Library of Congress Control Number:
2014936441

A FREE eBook edition is available
with the purchase of this print book

CLEARLY PRINT YOUR NAME IN THE BOX ABOVE

Instructions to claim your free eBook edition:
1. Download the BitLit app for Android or iOS
2. Write your name in UPPER CASE in the box
3. Use the BitLit app to submit a photo
4. Download your eBook to any device

Original Artwork by:
Melanie Watrous
sbquaker@aol.com

Photography by:
Justine Wichael
justinewichael@gmail.com

Cover Design by:
Rachel Lopez
www.r2cdesign.com

Interior Design by:
Bonnie Bushman
bonnie@caboodlegraphics.com

In an effort to support local communities, raise awareness and funds, Morgan James Publishing donates a percentage of all book sales for the life of each book to Habitat for Humanity Peninsula and Greater Williamsburg.

Get involved today, visit
www.MorganJamesBuilds.com.

Habitat
for Humanity®
Peninsula and
Greater Williamsburg
Building Partner

To Eric, who has always
supported me in all my dreams.

Contents

Introduction   **xi**

    Who is this book's reader?   *xi*

    The Problem   *xii*

    Why I Had to Write a Book   *xiii*

    A Different Kind of Book on Infidelity   *xiv*

    It works!   *xiv*

    There is hope.   *xv*

    Some Thoughts before We Begin   *xvi*

Chapter 1   **Signs, Evidence, and What to Do with It All**   **1**

    Inklings of Infidelity   *2*

    Go with your gut.   *4*

    Getting Confirmation   *12*

    *What **is** an affair, anyway?*   *15*

Should I confront my betrayer?   16

Permission, Envision, Decision   20

Ask Yourself   23

Chapter 2   Confront or Keep Quiet   **24**

Timing   24

Laying It All Out There   26

Possible Responses   27

Now what?   29

How Things Might Turn Out   33

What questions am I allowed to ask?   34

Exercise: How to Structure an
      Information-Gathering Session   37

Ask Yourself   38

A Final Caution   38

Chapter 3   I've Been Cheated On. Now What?   **39**

It's Confirmed . . .   39

What's normal?   40

So Many Feelings   43

Whom to Tell   47

Don't rewrite history.   51

Grieving   52

DO NOT MAKE A DECISION!   57

Exercise: Dealing with the Questions of Others   59

So what's next?   61

Ask Yourself   63

Chapter 4	**"You Want Me to *What*?"**	**66**
	New Rules	*67*
	How Things Might Turn Out	*70*
	Ask Yourself	*73*
Chapter 5	**Back to a Seminormal Life**	**74**
	Some Common Concerns	*75*
	A Caution against Becoming a Victim	*77*
	What if he's staying with me	
	just because he "has to"?	*79*
	The Tricky Part of Trust	
	(the Second Time Around)	*79*
	Giving the Relationship an Honest Evaluation	*83*
	Ask Yourself	*83*
Chapter 6	**"How Could You!"**	**85**
	Who cheats?	*85*
	So why do affairs happen?	*89*
	What makes one relationship	
	more vulnerable than another?	*95*
	How Unspoken Expectations	
	Can Contribute to an Affair	*101*
	"I love you, but I'm not in love with you."	*106*
	Other Contributors to Infidelity	*109*
	Going Forward	*111*
	Ask Yourself	*112*
	Exercise: What are your ideas and expectations	
	for love and relationships?	*112*

Chapter 7   **So What Was *Your* Part in All This?**   **114**

Envision the Conversation   *115*

Now what do we do?   *119*

What's next?   *125*

Ask Yourself   *126*

Chapter 8   **Decisions and Forgiveness (Yes, It's Required)**   **127**

Signs that Maybe It's Time to Go   *128*

Choosing to Stay for "the Other Reasons"   *129*

He still doesn't know what he wants.   *132*

You don't want the relationship

(but thought you did).   *134*

Forgiveness (Oh, no, not that!)   *135*

Afterword   **The End of the Journey:**   **145**

Stepping Out Together in the

New Relationship You Both Have Created   *145*

About the Author   **147**

Endnotes   **149**

Introduction

According to some studies, nearly half of us will experience infidelity in a relationship. According to others, it may be as many as three-fourths of us. Harsh, I know, but those are the stats. Are you part of those numbers? Would you know it if you were? Do you know the secrets to finding out, and if you do find out, do you know where to go from here?

Who is this book's reader?

I have long wanted to write a book for people who experience this devastating event. For fourteen years, I've sat in my chair as a therapist and heard all the heartrending stories . . .

A tall, handsome man in his mid-fifties, married to the same woman for twenty-three years, was blissfully in love.

Then his world blew up when his wife told him she was in love with his best friend.

And what about the woman who has it all: a stay-at-home mom, financially secure, with three beautiful children? One day, she does the laundry and finds a love note from her husband's mistress. Now she's divorced and working to support her children, who are in day care. Meanwhile, her husband has "upgraded" to a new life with a new wife.

Then there's the young, beautiful girl who falls for the guy who has cheated on every other girlfriend. He'll be faithful, he assures her, because she's different. Well, within months, she stumbles upon the fact that she wasn't so different after all.

This is the awful truth for most of the people who sit in my office. Imagine the shock, the brokenness. In a single moment, your happily-ever-after has plunged over the falls and dashed itself on the rocks below. Your entire vision for your life is shattered.

So . . . what now? You have no idea. Do you kick your betrayer out? Go to therapy? Forgive and forget after tearful reassurances that it will never, *ever* happen again? As you reel from this bombshell, you are left grasping at straws, not knowing what to do or how to go on living.

The Problem

Statistics show that many therapists who work with couples dealing with infidelity tend to focus primarily on the *relationship* and not the *affair*. Fifty-nine percent of couples said their therapist mainly focused on general marital problems, not the affair. And 23 percent said their therapist encouraged them to quickly cover the highlights of the affair, then move on.[1] Prematurely focusing on the relationship and overlooking the betrayal is one of the biggest mistakes that therapists make when trying to counsel a couple dealing with infidelity. This type of one-size-fits-all treatment usually leads to minimizing the betrayal as "just an event" to be forgiven and forgotten. But it's never *just* an event. This glossing-over of betrayal hinders rather than helps both the individuals and the relationship.

The treatment of infidelity involves many specific issues that *must be addressed* if we are to get the best possible outcome for the people involved. If those who are trying to provide counseling don't understand these issues, counseling can leave both the couple and the individual feeling hurt, angry, and hopeless.

Why I Had to Write a Book

I couldn't bear to hear one more client describe her many attempts to get help dealing with her partner's infidelity—only to end up feeling worse than ever. I was frustrated with the stories of couples who sought counseling for the affair but found no improvement even after months of therapy. Many of these people were now in my office as a last resort after several failed attempts at therapy for either their marriage or themselves. I salute every one of them for their courage. They didn't give up but instead chose to give therapy one more chance.

A Different Kind of Book on Infidelity

I wanted to write a book that would be user friendly for anyone who has had to face a partner's infidelity. I wanted to provide a guide that you can pick up the moment you find out about—or even suspect—an infidelity. I want you to know what to do and where to go as well as how to confront your partner and what steps need to be taken for him to earn back your trust. Being armed with information and direction is empowering. That is why I also created the Web site www.therapydiva. com. I wanted to provide a resource that women could access RIGHT NOW, during that fragile time when they initially suspect or discover betrayal.

I wanted to offer a guide for a woman who wants easy-to-follow steps, lists of questions to ask her partner and herself, and easy-to-implement exercises to help her make decisions about the relationship moving forward. I didn't want to create another book filled with theory and psychobabble that you have to cut through when you just need answers and direction *right now*. I didn't want chapters filled with other people's stories for you to sift through when you are just looking for some direct answers.

It works!

The methods in this book have given many women and couples the guidance they needed to navigate their way through the minefield that is infidelity. The methods' success is measured not by how many couples stay together, but by how confident each woman feels in the end about her decisions. She is at peace with what has happened, and goes forward with the hope of loving and trusting again, whether in her current relationship or in the next.

I intend for this book to help validate, encourage, and better equip the woman who has been incorrectly told, "Don't ask questions; just forgive and forget, move on, and find out what you did wrong." I specifically refer to women because they are the ones I primarily work with. The men who are in my office are typically the spouses of my clients. I hope my book finds its way into the hands of that couple who desperately want to make things better but are stuck going in endless circles, either from therapy or from just trying to figure it all out by themselves. This book is written to women, but it is also for the couple desiring to restore the relationship. It provides thought-provoking questions to help them understand why the affair happened, and it gives exercises for the couple at each stage of dealing with the infidelity. The hopeful truth is that 70 percent[2] of couples survive an affair and usually come out stronger in the end.

There is hope.

I am writing these words because I want to tell you, there is hope. I want to tell you that someday it will not feel as horrible as it does today. Whether or not you decide to stay in this relationship, you *can* go forward and be stronger in the end. Right now you may feel the dread of never being able to trust anyone again. Fine, that's perfectly understandable. But this fear doesn't have to stay a part of your life forever. That frightened voice that warns you never to let another person into your life and your heart again doesn't have to block you from ever having another relationship.

This new discovery of betrayal now has you looking through a microscope at every relationship in your life, for the least sign of unfaithfulness. All relationships are now in question. This is your new reality. After all, if the person you trusted most in all the world could betray you, why shouldn't it be the same with everybody else?

When you find out you've been betrayed, you just want to curl up into a ball, stay home, and never deal with the outside world again. You have no idea how you will ever face another day, or how to start picking up the pieces and just have a normal life again. Whom can you tell? What will they think of you? What if you decide you want to stay? How will your friends and family respond if you decide to leave?

All these are normal questions that everyone has when they have been betrayed. And now, together, we are going to figure out how you can make the decision to stay or to go, and how you can move on and have healthy relationships in the future. You will learn to *love without fear.*

Some Thoughts before We Begin

In this book, I use the following terms to refer to the actions and events that have led to broken trust in the relationship: "affair," "cheating," "infidelity," and "betrayal." I call the person who was unfaithful "your partner" or the "betrayer." The person your partner became involved with is his "lover," and you are the "betrayed." I make a point of using the many terms that refer to infidelity in our culture today, so that you can hear the message of this book in familiar language. I define an affair as *going outside the relationship to get one's relational needs met.*

Ultimately, this book is for the woman wanting to explore the possibility of restoring the relationship after infidelity. I do not have an agenda for the one betrayed either to stay in the relationship or to move on. Rather, I am here to walk alongside the woman who was betrayed, and guide her through the process of dealing with infidelity, by providing exercises, information, and questions that pave the way for a well-considered decision to stay or to go.

And finally, I want to say "thank you" to my many clients who have taught me so much about this difficult journey through infidelity. Throughout the book, I have referred to some of them and their situations, though I have changed various details to protect their privacy.

Chapter 1

Signs, Evidence, and What to Do with It All

So what are some of the clues that you should have been looking for? Is it possible to know *ahead of time* what to look for? Should you have known that you were being cheated on? Or maybe you're wondering whether your partner is cheating on you now.

Wouldn't it be nice to have a list of red flags to look for? Well, it just so happens that most people who are cheating do tend to have certain behaviors in common. If you have already gone through the horrible, gut-wrenching experience of finding out you've been cheated on, first of all, please DON'T

BLAME YOURSELF for not knowing. I mean, who goes into a relationship thinking they're going to be cheated on? It's a common understanding that this is not how we treat those we love.

There's no reason why you should have spent every day going through a checklist in your mind, trying to make sure that your partner was committed to you. Remember that annoying saying that "hindsight is 20/20." Well, as you read through these clues, those moments will come when you hit yourself on the forehead and think, *of course! How could I miss that!* That's okay. The trick will be not to blame yourself for not seeing what seems so painfully obvious now. I promise you, beating yourself up for it won't help. So when that moment of crystal-clear hindsight comes, and you find yourself going down the road of blaming yourself, *pause,* right where you are, and applaud yourself for taking the chance to trust. This is important because it's a risk that so many people won't let themselves be vulnerable to. You can—and *should* be able to— believe that when two people commit to each other, both will stand by their word.

Inklings of Infidelity

Infidelity does not follow a specific and predictable path. Wouldn't that be nice, though? I find that cheaters fall into either of two groups. One is the group of people who will do *anything* to hide the fact that they are cheating. Then we have the other group, who, even though they are cheating, are struggling. They want to come clean, to get out from under the stress of the lies. But they don't, because they fear what will happen when their partner finds out. They also vacillate about whether they want to continue in the affair.

Yes, I know, this second type of person seems crazy. After all, why continue the affair if it's a source of stress? The fact is, they often *hope they will be found out,* so they can end the lie. But they aren't strong enough to do it on their own, so they want someone else to give them a reason to stop lying.

It's funny how, as people, the way we behave and the way we feel don't always line up. We seem to be experts at saying yes to a situation, even knowing the dangers, but when we find ourselves in the midst of danger, we don't know how to get out of it.

For some cheaters, being found out is the avenue they can use to end their marriage. Rather than hurt their partner by listing all the reasons why they are unhappy, they figure it might just be easier to be found out as a cheater. Yes, it's frustrating that someone wouldn't even have the strength of character just to tell you what's going on. So instead, they choose to address a troubled relationship by engaging in one of the most harmful, hurtful behaviors imaginable.

Some people want to be found out, because they want their partner to be jealous. They figure that if their partner sees that someone else desires them, the partner will then find them more desirable. Yes, I know—it's a risky way to get those results. But people do it.

Now, as I go through the list of common behaviors of a cheater, it's important to realize that just because your partner is doing one of these things—or even two or three of these things—does not necessarily mean they are cheating on you.

You can't determine that someone is cheating, based on one behavior. Instead, you want to look for *patterns* in your partner's behavior. Do you see a shift, or departure, from their normal behavior and routines? These are the things you want to be on the lookout for. Any sudden change in another person's behavior usually has some meaning or reason behind it. Your goal is to see whether that change is because someone else has caught your partner's attention.

Go with your gut.

When clients of mine confide in me about an incidence (or incidences) of infidelity, more often than not they admit to having sensed that something was wrong before they knew for sure. Assuming you are not the type of person who interprets every little inconsistency as cause to suspect an affair, don't minimize your worry. Don't just dismiss it as "all in your mind." If, one day, something just doesn't feel right, you may want to keep an open mind—and open eyes. At least, be attuned to any of the following signs:

Privacy

Most obviously, one of the first things that happen when someone is cheating is that they begin to demand more privacy. For instance, they might start changing the time when they are on the computer. Maybe your partner stays on the computer well after you've gone to bed for the night. Or maybe, when you walk into the room and he's on the computer, he quickly shuts down the screen that he was on. You might notice that a computer or an e-mail account requires a password that was never needed before. Or maybe there's a new e-mail account that you don't recall seeing before.

These days, with all our smart phones and electronic notebooks, we can have many forms of messages: text messages, voice mail, e-mail. You may find an unexplained deletion of these messages. Or for some reason, phone call histories have been erased. In short, there is going to be a covering-up of anything that could lead to your finding out about the communication with the lover.

Curious Telephone Behavior

You might find it odd that your partner has a phone on hand all the time. I once had a client who told me her husband took the phone with him into the bathroom. What was happening, of course, was that her husband was turning on the shower and using the sound to muffle his conversation with his lover. Or he would text his lover while the shower was running, and make it seem as though he were just taking a long shower.

A partner with something to hide may not only constantly have their phone on him but may also seem *protective* of it. He may hesitate when you ask to use it just to make a call or snap a picture of the children playing.

You also may find that more phone calls are going to voice mail than before. If your partner is in the same room with you and sees that his lover is calling, he most likely will let that call go to voice mail. It will be especially noticeable since most people these days are tied closely to their phones. Many people hardly go five minutes without checking Facebook, texts, and

Twitter. So if someone who normally does respond suddenly lets a call or text go unaddressed, it should make you at least a little bit curious.

On the phone bill, you may see a number you don't recognize that's been called several times a day. It may be that these are not quick phone calls but are long in duration. Also, when you ask who this is, you may see your partner fumble to answer your question, or get angry at you for "checking up" on him. Here's a good rule of thumb: when somebody is doing something wrong and you ask them about what they're doing, their defensiveness should be a dead giveaway that this is something you need to look further into.

An increase in texting may also be a clue that someone else is grabbing their attention. They can even text a lover when they are in the same room as you, without your having a clue who they are talking to. A sudden increase in texting may suggest a budding romantic relationship.

Unscheduled Events

Most of us have very predictable schedules, with little variation. These schedules pertain to when we go to work, when we come home from work, when we work out, when we walk the dog. So if, all of a sudden, you find that your partner is staying at work later and saying that he's "swamped at work," or he has more dinner meetings than usual, that's something to look into. You might also notice that there are suddenly more conferences to be attended, more out-of-town travel, more weekend meetings. Work activities are some of the most often-used excuses to cover up the time spent with a secret lover.

Along with the change in schedule, if you start to ask questions about this, you usually get one of two behaviors: There's the person who gives overly detailed explanations. He's giving you names of projects, people he was with, minutiae about exactly what they were discussing, and so on. He's trying to convince you that this is a real thing that's going on. At the other end of the spectrum is the partner who just gives vague answers. He's going "out" or says he has a "meeting." When you ask questions about it, you get responses such as "You're not really interested" and "It's nothing you'd want to hear about." Or else, you get a defensive response, questioning why you re always bugging him about what he's doing.

Changes in Interest

If your partner has suddenly taken on a new hobby, sport, or other interest and it's something that you've never heard about before, there might be more to it. And if this new interest or activity is one that he doesn't want to share with you, or he gets defensive and says he wants to do "something by myself," that's usually not a good sign, either. This pretty well speaks globally about how most of us act when we get interested in somebody. We are suddenly interested in the same things they are. It's really no different when someone is cheating.

Personal Habits

Now, this is one of the more common and obvious ones. When someone loses a lot of weight, for example, they start to feel better about themselves. This new sense of self-worth can sometimes lead a person to begin exploring how they might relate to other people. Their confidence level may turn into more conversation or even flirtation with people they might not have approached before. Sometimes, it's hard to know which one came first: did your partner become interested in somebody else first, or did this new level of fitness increase their self-esteem to the point that they could see themselves being with another person? I see this situation often in my office. Weight loss, especially in women, precedes many affairs.

Sometimes, a change in a person's overall appearance can be a signal that something is afoot. Is the person wearing a new hairstyle or getting a new look? Is there a change in their personal style? Has their wardrobe suddenly gotten more updated? Perhaps they have become generally more concerned about their appearance than they were before. Once, I knew of a woman who would ask her husband to give his opinion on her outfit before she went out with her lover under the false pretense that she was going out with her girlfriends. How sad that he was giving his approval of how great she looked, only for her to rendezvous with her lover! And while we're talking about clothing, an obvious topic is lingerie. If, all of a sudden, somebody who's been wearing granny pants pulls out a sassy Victoria's Secret number, that could be a sign of a problem. If your man suddenly goes from "tighty whities" to something colorful and silky, this may not be a good sign, either. Overall, a sudden preoccupation with looks should sound a warning bell.

The Money Trail

The use of money always carries clues to what is going in someone's personal life. One of the first indications that something is amiss may be that more money is going out than before. When you question this, you could meet with a defensive, hostile attitude. You may get a response of "Why are you asking me this, all of a sudden? I don't have to account to you for every dollar I spend!" Overall, there will be a general state of defensiveness around the sudden increase in spending. You might find that there are missing checks, with no explanation for what they were written for. You may notice questionable credit card charges. I once had a woman client whose husband commuted often. Thus, she was used to seeing charges at restaurants for meetings or when he was out of town. Then suddenly, she noticed a dramatic increase in restaurant charges, and extremely high amounts spent elsewhere. This was what tipped her off to the fact that he was having his "evening meeting" meals with his lover. Now, why this man didn't think his wife would notice, since she was the one who paid the credit card bills, is quite beyond me. You may notice credit card charges for stores you don't often frequent. There's a more than passing chance that these places are where your partner's lover's gifts come from. Hotel stays, on the other hand, are usually paid for in cash, so you may see larger-than-normal withdrawals from the ATM.

Relationships at Home

When people are engaged in an extramarital relationship, it affects everyone in the home. Specifically, I'm talking about the children. Your partner may be angrier or more impatient with them all of a sudden or may forget details that are typically routine, like bringing your daughter to dance class or soccer practice, or your son to play rehearsal. It takes a lot of time and mental energy to create and maintain a secretive life. You may notice an increased awareness of time, and the duration of daily activities may cause your partner frustration, because he's busy watching the time to see when he can get away to call or see his lover. Any change in routine can frustrate him, since it may result in a missed opportunity to have contact with his lover. Your partner can hold together this secret relationship only so long before the other areas of life start to feel the pinch.

And there's also this whole other aspect of home life, which is so close it can be hard to see: how your partner is relating with *you*. To be suddenly critical of one's partner is a very common behavior among cheaters. When you're being compared to the person your partner is smitten with, you suddenly don't look so appealing. You might even find your partner being critical just so he can start a fight with you and have an excuse to storm out of the house and "cool down," only to go see his lover.

On the other hand, a cheating partner can respond in the completely opposite way. He may overcompensate by being more complimentary than usual. He wants to give you the impression he is still attracted to you and happy in the relationship, so you won't wonder whether something's going on.

Sex and Affection

This is another of those areas prone to extreme behaviors. There may be an increase in sexual behavior because your partner has a more active libido from having more sex. He may be more passionate all of a sudden or may want to try out "new techniques" with you. Now, let's remember to keep some perspective here: just because your partner gets a little frisky or wants to experiment in bed doesn't mean he's having an affair. Still, if it's a sudden change in behavior that you haven't experienced with them before, something else may be behind it. So it's not necessarily true that someone having an affair responds by being *less* affectionate toward you.

At the other end of the cheating-behavior spectrum, we have the person who wants to avoid sex and affection altogether. You're going to see less of those spontaneous little affectionate behaviors. Whether it's holding hands, a peck on the cheek, or just the occasional "Good morning, beautiful!" it's often the small things that you'll see diminish.

Social Life

If you and your partner have typically gone to parties together, gone out to dinner with other couples, or met friends for a drink or a movie, and those things suddenly quit happening as much, that's not good. If your spouse tells you, "You don't have to come to my boring office party," when you've gone every other year, that should also give you pause. Sometimes, the lover may actually get angry when she finds out your partner is doing "normal" life activities with you. *She* gets jealous of *your* relationship with *her* lover.

"We're just friends."

"We're just friends" is a line that gets a lot of use. We don't seem to catch on that this is one of the most incriminating sentences a spouse or partner could ever utter. Without even realizing it, your partner may talk about another person more often. He brings up someone's name with unusual frequency or seems to know an awful lot of details about someone's life. When you ask why this person's name keeps coming up, you may get a defensive response or—just as bad—the old "Don't worry, we're just friends." He will assure you in the most convincing voice that you have absolutely nothing to worry about. If he has to say they're "just friends," they probably aren't.

Now, here's the biggie . . .

A recent survey by Todd Shackelford and David Buss showed 170 of the most typical behaviors of a cheater.[3] And guess what one of the most predictive behaviors was: No more "I love you."

Those three syllables that hold so much meaning for all of us also convey much meaning by their absence. When your partner can no longer tell you he loves you, it's time to wake up and pay attention.

Now, let me reiterate once more: one, two, or even three of these behaviors do not necessarily mean that your partner is cheating on you. Remember, it's the pattern of sudden changes in behavior that you want to look for. Changes in life are good; changes cloaked in secrecy are not.

Getting Confirmation

To find out if your suspicions are correct, you may have to do a bit of detective work on your own. Here's a brief list of things that many people have done to find out if their partner was cheating. And right about now, before you read the list, a disclaimer is in order: I am not promoting or condoning any of these behaviors. I am merely reiterating ways that others have used to find out whether their partner was cheating.

Mileage

Typically, most people drive roughly the same number of miles from week to week. They go to work, come home, go to they gym, make a run to the grocery store, and so on. If you suddenly find that your partner's mileage is much more than it used to be, and it doesn't really jibe with where your partner has supposedly gone, this likely points to some new travel. You can also look at gas receipts. Take a look at the places where your partner is getting gas. If it doesn't seem to be on his normal daily route, you have to wonder. Also, if he's going to restaurants farther away from home than seems necessary, that could be to avoid bumping into someone he knows while trysting with his lover.

Keeping the Score

You can learn some surprising things just from counting contraceptive devices or sexual performance pills. Last time you looked, were there seven condoms in the case, or six? How many little purple pills in that Viagra bottle? (Or, worse yet, you may find Viagra pills when you weren't expecting to.) I had one man in my office say that his friend gave him a Viagra pill just so he could "try it out." But the interesting thing is, he never told his wife about it, and she never saw any change in his sexual performance. To add to the confusion, his wife didn't see any problem with his performance in the first place. A woman, too, can hide her contraception. She may have in her purse birth-control pills that she was not using before, or condoms that she isn't using with you.

Cell Phone Bills

This is a no-brainer, really. You can call your cell phone provider and have them fax you a list of phone numbers called or texted over a certain period of time. Again, the thing to watch for is a number that has been called multiple times and whose calls last a while. You may then want to call that number yourself and see who answers the phone. But before you do, remember, you are not going to say *anything*! In general, I suggest you not confront a lover. It rarely leads to anything good.

The Best Day of the Year to Catch a Cheater

Now, you're probably thinking that one day of the year is pretty much the same as another for trying to catch someone cheating on you. But there is one day with far and away the best odds. Yup, you got it: Valentine's Day! This is the day when everything is about love, romance, and flowers. Most people want to be with the person they love on that day. Remember back when you first fell in love? Valentine's Day was always an opportunity to express how you felt. It's no different when someone's cheating. There's that same giddy feeling of excitement and passion. They want to share that special day with their lover. You might find that a sudden business trip or late meeting crops up on February 14. Or a family emergency that simply *must* be attended to crops up on that particular evening. Anything to avoid spending this day of romance with somebody other than their lover!

Times of Opportunity

A cheater will tend to take advantage of having the house to himself. You might want to try coming home early (and unannounced) from a trip. You may want to show up and "surprise" your partner when he's on his business trip.

Hiring a Detective

When all else fails, if you think your partner may just be super sly at covering his tracks but you still think something's happening, hire a professional. Most people think this is somehow complicated or difficult to do or that it's going to cost a ton of money. Not true. There are plenty of ways to hire somebody who's willing to follow your partner around. And usually, they can quickly and easily uncover whether your partner is sneaking around. One of the best ways to find out whether your partner is cheating is to discuss with him that you are curious about his behavior. And when he promises you that absolutely nothing is going on, you suggest that you hire a detective just to make sure. If you get resistance on this issue, bingo! Anyone who will not agree to being followed or watched usually has something to hide.

What *is* an affair, anyway?

Too many people think it "doesn't count" as cheating if they didn't have sex. Wrong! It absolutely is still cheating. In fact, in some ways, sex is the least of it. You see, anytime someone ventures outside their relationship to get their needs met, that's cheating.

Let's say, for example, that someone is in a clandestine online relationship. Although they may not be having sex with their Internet love, they are talking, being vulnerable, and sharing intimate details about their lives with someone other than their partner. To add insult to injury, they might be "sexting" (exchanging sexual text messages) or having provocative phone or Internet conversations about sex with this person. In this situation, people are doing things that allow them to be involved sexually without actually engaging in physical sex acts. Well, guess what: it's still cheating.

What about the purely emotional affair? Where an individual is completely caught up and distracted with thoughts of another person. This is typical of a friendship or work relationship that slowly, gradually crosses the line. One begins to think about the other person all the time: looking forward to hearing from them, maybe even dressing in a certain way to get their attention. But there is no sexual element to the relationship. The real problem here is that they are more interested and invested in the other person than in their legitimate partner. This is where the betrayal begins. The cheater starts shutting out the partner because now someone else is meeting their emotional needs. This, too, is cheating.

There is also the scenario where the cheater *did* have sex, but it was a one-night stand. And yes, even if it happened only once, it's still cheating. Whether it's one night or a hundred, it is a betrayal. All three of these scenarios hurt just as bad as an ongoing sexual affair. There is no difference in the severity of pain; all betrayal hurts the same.

Should I confront my betrayer?

So now that you've gathered some evidence, it's time to ask yourself some questions. Does everything add up? Or are you mentally construing signs that point to something that isn't real? Let's say your partner has made several calls to the same number. You work up the courage to call this number, and someone answers, but you're not sure who it is. Do you use just that one piece of evidence to confront your partner and accuse him of having an affair?

If you don't have enough evidence and it turns out that your partner is *not* cheating, he's going to feel upset, even outraged. He'll wonder why you are checking up on him when he's done nothing wrong. I can't overstress the importance of having solid information if you're going to confront your partner. The more evidence you have, the better the odds of getting an honest response. So don't jump the gun with the first thing you find. A little bit of patience will pay off after you've gathered the right information. This is so important, I have to say it again: WAIT until you have enough information. I understand that it's tempting to confront your partner with the first bit of evidence you find. Your emotions will be running high, but don't act impulsively. Any indication that you are "checking up" on your partner will only warn him to cover his tracks better, making it that much harder for you to get further confirmation of his cheating.

So now here's the big question: What are you going to do? Will you even confront your partner?

Choosing Silence

At this point, you might say to yourself, *I don't know. Even with all the evidence, chances are, he's not cheating on me.* You might consider all the evidence and still not be able to come to terms with the fact that your partner is cheating on you.

So you make the choice to look the other way. You make this choice because . . .

- "I have a great life."
- "My partner is a great provider."
- "We have children together."
- "I'm scared I can't make it on my own"

Regardless of the reason, you *don't want* confirmation of the affair, because then you will have to acknowledge it. Your rationale is that it's worse to know for certain that your partner is cheating on you than simply to wonder. By deciding to learn the truth, all the while knowing that you will do nothing about it, you're almost giving him permission to keep cheating on you. Your silence allows you to keep up the appearance of maintaining your dignity.

In a slightly different scenario, you choose to carry on with life, denying the reality of an affair despite the mountain of evidence. In short, you choose denial. In this scenario, you choose to believe in that slim-to-nonexistent possibility that it didn't really happen. You hang on to that shred of hope that this is not really happening.

If either of the above scenarios describes your decision, allow me to make a couple of suggestions.

If you choose to acknowledge the evidence and not confront your partner, you need to consider how this is going to affect both you and your behavior. Are you going to make peace with the fact that your partner is unfaithful? By making peace with this choice and accepting the reality of your situation, you are also choosing to quit wasting time and energy on being suspicious, because at this point, it does you no good. You aren't going to confront your betrayer, so searching for additional confirmation will only prove emotionally exhausting and distressing. Acknowledging the *why* of your decision will allow you to move forward more peacefully, knowing that you made the best choice for *you, now.*

Choosing to Confront

If you are choosing to confront, I want you to prepare yourself mentally and emotionally for whatever response you may get from your partner. The response may well go something like this: "Yes, I've been cheating on you." I want you to be ready to hear those words. You need to prepare for how that is going to feel, and know how you're going to respond if that is the answer you get. Imagine again that he has said "yes." I always say to my clients, "I want you to anticipate the worst but hope for the best." What I do *not* want is for you to walk into that situation, find out that you have indeed been cheated on, and then sit there not knowing what to do.

If you do confront, I want you to envision all the possible scenarios and how you want to respond to them. Envision your partner confirming the infidelity. What will you do then? Envision him denying it. What will you do then? Envision a confirmation and then your partner telling you he wants to fix things. What will you do? What if he confirms and wants to end things? What if there is no doubt in your mind about the cheating and yet, he denies, denies, denies? You need to be prepared for every one of these scenarios to happen. There is no guaranteeing how this will all turn out.

Permission, Envision, Decision

Before moving any further, I want you to get familiar with a process I will refer to throughout the book. You will hear me say these three words over and over again as we go forward:

- *Permission*
- *Envision*
- *Decision*

This is a three- step process that will be of great help to you in almost any area of your life whenever you need to make an important choice. Whether it's getting married, having kids, applying for a job, not attending a family function, or, yes, dealing with infidelity, if you can learn how to apply these three steps, you will have greater ease and clarity in all your decision making.

Give yourself permission.

When you are making an important decision, I want you to start by giving yourself *permission* to make a choice that is right for you, regardless of how others may feel about it. You have permission to make what may, in the eyes of others, be a bad choice. You have permission to make an unpopular choice. You even have permission to make a *selfish* choice. So go ahead and remove all expectations that others have on you.

Now, I am not suggesting that you dismiss any counsel you receive from others, and make decisions in isolation. Absolutely not! But in my long experience as a therapist, most people do this part—getting advice and direction from others—quite well already. It's the next part that they struggle with: the part where you consider ALL the information and make the decision that works for you, REGARDLESS of how others might feel.

It is far too easy to get caught up in pleasing others, doing what you think they will approve of. But they aren't the one who has to live with your life decisions. Yes, maybe they will disapprove of your choice and walk away thinking you just made the worst choice of your life. They may even hold on to that opinion for a couple minutes or days. But then what? They go back to living their life, and you are no longer even a thought in their mind. They are not thinking about you and your choice nearly as much as you are. People tend to be self-interested by nature, so don't think they are going home and obsessing about your problems. (And if they are, guess what: that's *their* problem.)

It's easy to want the approval of others. But you need to weigh out the cost of that approval. To make a choice that does not serve you well, just so you can avoid feeling uncomfortable or disapproved of when you are in the presence of other people is a high price to pay.

Give yourself permission to let others down. Give yourself permission not to be who they want you to be. Give yourself permission to be genuinely yourself. Give yourself permission not to have it all figured out—even to make a mistake. Give yourself permission to get it wrong. It's all okay. You will survive. Being afraid to let others down and not live up to the expectations you *think* others have of you can hold you back from real freedom.

So go ahead. What do you need to give yourself permission to do?

Once you release the expectations that were limiting the available choices, you are now free to move forward with entertaining the idea of the decision that *you* deem best for your life. I now want you to picture your life playing out as a result of this choice.

Envision it.

How will your everyday life change as a result of that decision? How will your work life, family life, social life, emotional life change? What does it feel like when you envision a life resulting from this decision? Does it feel good? Do you see some new problems that might arise as a result of this decision? What adjustments will you need to make in your life as a result of that decision?

When you start to envision this, I want to you "sit with it" for a couple of days. Imagine over the next few days that you have made this decision. How will the decision be affecting you two days from now? Do you still feel good about that decision two days later? Can you stick with that decision, or do you see yourself wavering?

Once you have played out that choice in your mind and become comfortable with the idea of how your life will look as a result of that choice, it's time to decide.

Decide.

Your decision is now as informed and thought out as it can be, short of your actually living the choice. This doesn't mean there won't be surprises or that things will even turn out how you imagined, but what matters most is this: you didn't make a choice that was impulsive or driven by the desires of others. And in decision making, that, my dear, is a formula for success!

— Ask Yourself —

1. Looking back, were there any signs that you missed?
2. What do you think kept you from seeing those signs?
3. Are you going to choose silence?
4. If you are making this choice, why? List the reasons here:

Chapter 2

Confront or Keep Quiet

S o now you've gathered all the evidence and you're ready to confront your partner. Before you do this, though, you want to have all your information in one place. It would not be uncommon for your partner to challenge you with questions such as "How do you know?" or "Give me an example." I want you to be prepared so that when these questions come at you, you'll be ready with the proof.

Timing

The first thing I want you to think about is, *when* are you going to bring this up? You want to be careful about the timing. I don't want you to do it when your partner is getting ready for work and already feels rushed. You probably don't want to do it just before heading out for a social event, either. And you definitely don't want to do it when the children are up (if you have children). You probably don't want to do it while you're out in public, because it could get messy. And you probably don't want to do it late at night when both of you are tired after a long day.

So I'm going to suggest that you ask your partner when a good time would be to talk about "something that's been on your mind." This is a neutral way to let him know that you need to talk about something, without creating defensiveness and too much curiosity. Then pick a time when both of you are well rested and when you have a good chunk of time. I would say two to three hours. Now, the whole thing may last only five minutes because your partner could storm out and say that you're being ridiculous. But if it turns into a productive conversation where you can get some answers, you want to make sure you have enough time to do that. You're going to make sure there are no distractions and that you are emotionally ready to handle whatever response you get.

At this point, you may be thinking, "Why should I have to be so careful and gentle with how I confront my partner?" You're probably really angry. When you have finally made the decision to confront, your adrenaline is pumping and you want answers *now*! You might be questioning why, if he had so little regard for you when he cheated, you should have any more regard for him when you call him out on it.

Here's the reason: this stage of the healing process isn't about him. It's about *you*. I want you to have the best environment possible so you can get the best, most useful answers possible. You want this to go as smoothly as possible. I know that sounds weird—this confrontation going *smoothly?*—but you can certainly aim for it.

Laying It All Out There

You're going to present the information to him all at once. Don't hold anything back. You can get a much better response if you lay it all out right then. When faced with such overwhelming evidence, he may just decide that it's pointless trying to deny the affair. When all the information is right there in front of him, it's going to be a lot more difficult to tell you that you're "being crazy" or that "it's just in your head."

My only suggestion here is that you give the information in stages during this initial confrontation. By the end of this conversation, you will have shared all the information to your partner, *but in increments that make sense.*

For example, if you ask your partner about a phone number you find being texted often and he says he has no idea who it is, you follow with the identity of the person you have managed to figure out. Say he then comes up with an excuse saying, "Oh, yeah, I did have to talk to So-and-so a lot; it was about work." Of course, you know that the conversations were *not* about work, so you then reveal the screen shot of a text message that proves they were talking about quite a bit more than work. You want to confront with all your information, but first, find out how forthcoming he's going to be, by giving him the opportunity to come clean from the get-go.

Possible Responses

Denial and Defensiveness

One of the responses you may get, of course, is denial. Now, you might have a really crafty partner who can talk his way out of anything. He will find a way to explain away every single thing you found, and make you feel as though you've got it all wrong and that you must be crazy to think he would ever cheat on you. Don't buy it! Do not let this denial response derail you. If you have all this information in front of you, and it all points to one conclusion, then you can be pretty sure you're not being crazy. So ask yourself, "Is it really possible that every single one of these things has a legitimate explanation other than that my partner is cheating on me?"

Here's one way to look at it: if a friend came to you and presented all this information she found in her relationship, what would your thoughts be? You will be easily convinced by your partner's explanations because, let's face it: you want to believe that your partner has been completely faithful to you. Do not let this wish overcome your desire for the truth. Remember, the truth is what sets you free. Everything short of that just keeps you trapped.

Relief at Ending the Cover-Up

Another response you may get from your partner is relief. What started out as maybe a "one-night stand" or "innocent flirting" may have gotten away from him. This relationship that moved from friendship to an intimate/emotional/sexual relationship may have begun to take on a life of its own without your partner's ever really intending it to happen. The ongoing lies, the covering up—all this can be quite stressful. When some betrayers find out that you know, it comes as a huge relief to them.

You may be sitting here scratching your head at this response, thinking, if this was such a huge stress, why didn't your partner just end it or come clean sooner? While your partner probably can't explain—and most likely wouldn't (at least, not in any fashion acceptable to you)—the response I want you to attend to is the relief. In some cases, this is actually a good sign.

Relief at Ending a Bad Marriage

On the other hand, some people are relieved that their partner found out they're cheating, because it helps them end a bad relationship. Yes, this is a pathetic, cowardly way to end things, but it happens all the time. This is the kind of person who doesn't feel strong enough to let his partner know he's unhappy. So he chooses cheating as an easier exit plan than spending a few moments of uncomfortable honesty with you.

Remorse and Repentance

This, of course, is the most hopeful response. This is the one where the betrayer says, "Yes, you're right." He confirms your suspicions. And better yet, he is truly sorry.

The ironic thing about cheating is that when people are doing it, they don't realize that it's one of the most selfish behaviors they can choose to do. While they are caught up in the emotion and secrecy of it (along with the adrenaline rush), they are completely self-absorbed. Small wonder—after all, cheating is all about self-gratification.

If your partner comes clean, says he's sorry, and tells you he wants to end the affair and move on, great! You are one of the lucky few who can begin to heal and deal with the betrayal sooner rather than later. As painful as it is to get confirmation of the horrible truth, getting a remorseful and repentant response is far and away the best start you can possibly get.

Now what?

After the confrontation and the confession (repentant or not), what are you to do? You are going to have a lot of questions that you want answers to. And it is now time to go ahead and start the question-asking process.

This stage of dealing with the affair is crucially important. You MUST NOT SKIP IT! I am still amazed at the incorrect thinking that goes on in otherwise intelligent people. They hold that gathering information will only cause more hurt to the betrayed. They have this notion that you just need to move on and forgive and not get caught up in the details. Well, to that, I say, "Poppycock!" All I can deduce is that this sort of harebrained thinking must come from someone who has never been cheated on.

All reality as you knew it has come into question. Nothing stands as self-evident anymore. Cheating cleared the table, and now you need—and deserve!—confirmation across the whole board. The questions you have for your partner are many and important.

Information gathering can be comforting. There is a regained sense of control over an out-of-control situation. We naturally seek details and information to help us process and make sense of traumatic events. It will help if your partner can understand this perspective as it pertains to your healing process.

Ground Rules for Asking Questions

Now that you're both on the same page and it's out in the open that cheating has been going on, it's time to get answers to some of the questions you have. You should feel free to ask all the questions you need to ask, and you should expect truthful answers. This is a crucial part of your healing. I'm sure there's a part of you that really cringes at hearing the truth. Every answer can feel like a fresh stab in your heart. But then, there's this other part of you that knows you need to hear the truth, gory details and all.

What to Pay Attention to

When you start asking the questions, I want you to use the same rules that were set up when you confronted your partner about the cheating. This is a very important part of the process. The way that you go about asking questions can either make this stage tolerable and productive or make your partner angry and defensive and shut down any communication that might lead to some answers.

Timing for the Questions

I'm going to suggest that you talk to your partner about a good time that you can sit (notice that I say "sit," not "stand over," "yell at," or "get out the dueling pistols") together, just the two of you. No distractions—just your partner listening to you and answering questions honestly and openly.

Your Partner's Response

Your partner is not going to want to do this. He is absolutely going to *hate* this idea and will become ridiculously nervous about doing it. But look at it this way: this is the minimal pain that he has to go through for what he has done to you. One suggestion that might ease his situation a bit is for you to acknowledge his discomfort and tell him you appreciate that he is willing to do this to help you heal.

Question-and-Answer Time

You will probably go through this question-and-answer "event" multiple times. Make it quite clear that this is not going to be a one-time event. What usually happens is that you ask questions, get answers, then go away and process that information. This, then, leads to your having more questions.

When I see clients in my office and we go through this question-and-answer phase, it can often go on for several sessions. I appreciate their wanting to wait until our counseling sessions so they can have a healthy and safe environment to do the question-and-answer process. My hope is that after practicing this in a nonthreatening environment and being productive in the communication, they can transfer those skills to their talks at home.

After the first round of questions, you may be ready to go back at it again in a couple of days. In the meantime, write down the questions to be addressed during the next mutually agreed-upon session. Hold off on the questions until then. You do *not* have permission to rattle off questions any old time they come to mind. You will need to exercise self-control with this. Continue to follow this format of a mutually agreed time for this exercise.

It's going to be important for you to count on having these opportunities to ask questions. It's going to be equally important that your partner not feel as though he could be bombarded with your questions at any moment, day or night. That will only make him angry and resistant to giving you answers. You want to resist the urge, even though you're probably going to feel it many times a day, to shoot a text, send an e-mail, make a phone call, or fire a question while you're in the house together. I cannot express this strongly enough: you need to hold off and have a structured time to do this. Any other time is off limits.

The other reason it's so important for you to limit the days and the amount of time you spend doing this is that you can very quickly begin to define your relationship exclusively by "the betrayal." It's amazing how infidelity can become the overarching theme of your entire relationship at this point. This is completely understandable. After all, you spend maybe 80 percent of your day thinking about this, ruminating on it. You picture things all day. It's in your head all the time. The problem—and the danger—with this is that if you are not controlled about the information gathering and just focus on the betrayal, you forget all that is actually good in the relationship.

How long?

Your partner needs to know that this could go on for a while. You may have question-and-answer sessions for three months, six months, nine months. The hope is that the more honest your partner can be, the more quickly you can get through these information-gathering sessions. He needs to know that omitting information and avoiding answers is only going to extend the process. You will just "know" when something doesn't add up and you need to know more.

Your partner might tell you that you shouldn't know certain pieces of information, because it's just going to hurt you even more. You just correct him and explain that it's like a puzzle: you are driven to take the pieces of information and get them to fit together. You want to know what the whole picture looks like. He has to let you do this.

How Things Might Turn Out

The hope is that as you get the information you need, these question-and-answer sessions will become fewer and farther between. In the beginning, it will be completely emotional and raw. You both are going to feel emotionally and physically exhausted. You may not be able to sleep at night. You may not be able to eat. You may feel as though you don't know which end is up anymore. That's okay! This is a completely normal response to finding out all this information.

When to Stop Asking Questions and Gathering Information

At some point, you must decide that you have all the information you need, and choose to move on to the next phase of healing. Let your partner know that there will come a time when you both agree that the question-asking process is over. There has to be a moratorium on the information-gathering part. In my experience, this is one of the important things that people most often fail to do, and it results in more anguish and distress than necessary.

You and your partner will mutually agree to end the question-asking sessions, and information gathering will be over. If you make this decision and then, months later, start on it again, it will feel like finding out for the first time all over again. You will be choosing to open up the door and invite all those same initial feelings of hurt, betrayal, and shame back in. This is not to say that you won't have questions pop into your mind. You will. But I'm going to ask that you *not* give yourself permission to continue gathering information after the decision to end the questioning is in place.

This is important for another reason, too. There are very specific phases in healing and dealing with betrayal. The behaviors and the steps taken in each phase are very different. It's important that you respect both yourself and your partner. So when you say, "I know enough," stick to that decision.

What questions am I allowed to ask?

As I mentioned before, you should be able to ask whatever questions come to mind. You might want to know:

- How often did they have sex (if they did)?
- How often did they talk online?
- Where did they meet?
- How long has this relationship been going on?
- Who else knows about it?
- Was he really on a business trip when he said he was?
- Was he really working late?

And so on . . .

You're going to have a whole list of questions that feel vitally necessary to ask. Before you start asking, here is one very important suggestion:

Don't get specific on sexual details!

Professionals are split in their opinions on this. I think you need to know everything—everything, that is, *except* specific sexual details. The images that you're going to create in your mind are going to be torturous. The next time you have sex with your partner, all you will be able to picture are the specific sexual behaviors that went on between your partner and his lover. This is not to say that you're not going to worry anyway or feel you are being compared. You may be wondering how this is any different from asking for other specific details earlier. It's been my professional experience that more often than not, these details hinder rather than help the healing process.

So please, heed my words of caution: however tempted you may be, don't go there! The thoughts and images in your mind are going to be bad enough already. Somehow, having them confirmed makes it that much worse.

I want you to be very thoughtful about the questions you ask. Once something is said, you can't unsay it. I want you to imagine hearing the answers to some of the questions you have. Think what it might feel like to know for certain. Do you *really* want to know *everything*? Are there only a few things that you feel certain you must know? I want to caution you to be very intentional in this information-gathering time. Just because there is information to be had doesn't mean you must know it in order to heal or make a decision. If your partner is going to be fully honest, be fully aware of what you think you need to know.

Your Partner's Job

When you ask questions, your partner is not allowed to justify or defend ANYTHING. All he gets to do is give you information. This is strictly an information-gathering session. There will be plenty of time later for your partner to discuss what was going on in his mind.

As you go through this grueling process of questions and answers, your betrayer has one job, which is to say, "I'm sorry." No explanations, no justifications, no excuses. Just plain and simple "I'm sorry."

This is so important, I'll say it again: **Your partner's only job is to say, "I'm sorry."**

It might look like this: You ask a question; he gives an answer; you get upset. He says, "I'm sorry." This cycle will repeat itself over the next few months as you respond to the pain of the betrayal.

At this point, it doesn't matter whether you even believe him. This is his job: to acknowledge the pain he caused you, regardless of the reasons behind it.

—Exercise—
How to Structure an Information-Gathering Session

- Both you and your partner agree to a time to sit down and address some questions you have about the infidelity.
- You make a list of the questions you have, while bearing in mind the reason you want specific information. Don't get specific about sexual details.
- In between these sessions, keep a record of further questions that come to mind, but DO NOT try to get answers outside the sessions.
- Try to stick to information gathering as opposed to asking for justification or explanations. This part will happen a little later.
- When you receive an answer, you are allowed to share how hurt, angry, sad, and humiliated you feel in response to your partner's previous behavior.
- Your partner is allowed to answer only with responses that express remorse and empathy. NO JUSTIFICATIONS.
- After you feel you have the answers you need, you both agree to put an end to the information-gathering sessions.

—Ask Yourself—

1. Have you had a question-and-answer session? If not, what is preventing that from happening?
2. Have you gotten all the information you need already? If so, have you made the agreement to end the question asking? If not, what prevents you from doing this?
3. Are you mistaking the permission to ask questions for a way to gain some sense of control over the infidelity?

A Final Caution

Sometimes, this freedom to ask for information provides the illusion that you have some sort of control over an uncontrollable situation. Don't buy the false sense of power and control you feel when you can ask questions. This may encourage you to continue the questioning longer than necessary, because it makes you feel in control. This is not a healthy way to give yourself reassurance or to prevent an affair from happening again.

Chapter 3

I've Been Cheated On.
Now What?

It's Confirmed . . .

You now know that the person you love has betrayed you in the most horrible way imaginable. You thought everything was fine. You have been blindsided—you had no idea this was coming. You knew that your relationship wasn't perfect, but nothing led you to believe that your partner would *cheat* on you. When you have confirmation that you've been cheated on, it feels as if your world has blown up in your face.

Feel free to explore what you need to do to digest this information about the betrayal. Don't stuff your feelings and put on the brave face. You will have to do this soon enough when facing the demands of a normal day. But for now, give yourself permission to leave the cooking and the laundry, to sit on the couch and stare, to cry. Or you might want to do the opposite and start a new project or finish an old one. All this is normal.

So what do you do now? How do you even begin to process this information? There is no correct way to grieve the loss of a relationship that was built on trust. This is probably one of the most emotionally messy processes you could possibly have to endure. So I'm going to tell you what you're likely to experience and how to handle it.

What's normal?

Many people, when they find out they've been cheated on, wonder if they're behaving normally. Lots of feelings and emotions go on when this happens. Finding out that something this awful has happened will leave your emotions all over the place. I often tell my clients, "Just expect that you won't be yourself for a while." I tell them to give themselves permission not to be who they typically are expected to be. It might be good to tell the people really close to you that you're probably not going to be up to doing some of the things you typically do.

For many, it feels as though the world had ground to a halt. Everything that you did effortlessly, without even thinking, now seems like a chore. Getting out of bed, eating, going to work, even taking care of yourself, can feel like drudgery.

You have permission to "check out."

So I want you to know right now that you have permission to "check out" emotionally for a while. I want you to remove all expectations on yourself. Take advantage of your sick days at work if you have to. It would be unrealistic to expect your mind to be focused on your job when you've got all this just rolling around in your head. You will need time to recover and find your way out of this dark emotional hole.Give yourself permission to check out socially for a little while. The thought of having to gather with other people and discuss trivial matters when your heart is broken is just way too much right now. But let me throw in a little caveat here: this doesn't give you permission to be antisocial for weeks and months. Of course it's fine, *for a short time,* not to feel up to social chitchat. If you just feel as though you can't keep some of the obligations you've made, that's okay. If you need to outsource daily duties such as cooking and cleaning the house, that's okay, too. There's no prescribed right way to deal with these first days, weeks, and months. What I'm asking you to do is sit still, think about what you feel capable of right now, and require only that of yourself.

You have permission to be on an emotional roller coaster.

You are going to vacillate between feelings of terrible anger and deep sadness. Your emotions will be all over the place. Give yourself permission to be all over the place, because that's what happens. You are going to sit and cry and wish that things could go back to the way they were. You're going to hope this is all just a bad dream that you're going to wake up from. You're going to grieve the fact that your partner was not 100 percent committed to you. At times, you will want nothing so much as for him to put his arms around you and tell you this was the worst thing he ever did and that all he wants is you.

Minutes later, you'll want to scream at him. You feel disgust at the very mention of his name and want him to be as far away from you as possible. Every time you look at him, all you can think of is how much he hurt you. His very presence is just a reminder of the hole he has blown in your heart. You love him, but you hate him. You need him and despise him. Don't be shocked when you want to hug him and then slap him, all in the same minute.

This is a cycle that will go on for some time. It goes up; it goes down. So I want you to think of it as a roller coaster. You will have your ups and your downs and your times when you are just cruising along. And in time, your highs and lows will not be as extreme as they are right now. But just as when you're on a real roller coaster, don't resist. Go along for the ride, and let yourself experience all the different emotions. Don't try to stifle what you are feeling. Your body has a way of knowing when you're upset, whether or not you give voice to it. People who ignore their feelings (and even some who don't) get upset stomach, headaches, jaw tension, tension in the neck and other body parts, body aches, and even panic attacks. So for the sake of your sanity and your health, please, let yourself feel.

But I don't like to cry.

Some people (a lot, actually) don't feel comfortable sharing their emotions. For whatever reason, crying or getting angry just doesn't serve any purpose that they can see, or at the very least, it's extremely uncomfortable and out of character for them. If you're that type of person, it's okay. I understand that your way of dealing is just to continue with life the way it was before. Your need for consistency and predictability in your day is your way to finding comfort and managing your pain. Your way of coping is not wrong. What I do want you to watch, though, is that you don't let your characteristic way of dealing with emotional pain lead to avoidance and denial.

There's a big difference between not letting a betrayal take over your life and completely avoiding thinking about it, because it's just too painful. Only you will know if this is what you are doing. So I want to encourage you to take some time at the end of each day, or at some point during the day, to really let yourself be still and feel. You don't have to yell and scream. You don't have to cry. But allow yourself to process the emotions that are going on in your body and your mind. We don't all look the same when we grieve the loss of a trusting relationship. The important part is that we allow ourselves to feel and process the pain and to grieve.

So Many Feelings

You may experience some depression, anxiety, or even panic. I say this not to scare you but to let you know that this reaction is normal and that other people who have been cheated on have also gone through this same emotional process. Here are some explanations and tips to use as you navigate through all the emotions related to the betrayal.

PTSD?

Many people have a response similar to post-traumatic stress disorder, or PTSD. This is a response that follows a traumatic experience such as war, kidnapping, a violent attack, earthquake, flood, car accident, and so on. Well, as it happens, you, too, have just had a traumatic experience. I have actually had clients who were soldiers and went to war tell me that handling the tragic events of war was actually *easier* than the pain of the affair. It's interesting that the experience of betrayal can actually create the same physical, mental, and emotional response as war.

So . . . what does PTSD look and feel like? You might have nightmares and feel fearful. Your sleep might be disturbed for some time. You may find that your mind races with thoughts and questions about the affair. You feel almost consumed by these thoughts. You may experience anxiety and do anything to avoid reminders associated with the betrayal. You may have flashbacks (feeling as if the event were happening again). You may be angry and irritable.

Flashbacks

After discovering that your partner has been cheating on you, you may find yourself "flashing back" to that scene. You could have flashbacks of the day that you confronted him, or of what was happening at the moment you realized that you had been cheated on. Some of these flashbacks can be *intrusive,* meaning that they pop up at the most inconvenient times. You could be driving down the road and have a flashback. Or you may be sitting in the middle of a meeting at work and have a flashback. If this happens, first of all, know that you are not going crazy. This response is completely normal, and there are effective ways to handle this distressing event.

When a flashback happens, you're just going to try your best to remain calm. Your body may want to panic. You may feel your heart start to race. It may be harder to breathe. This is what we call a panic attack. So it may be that your flashback sets off a panic attack. Do your best to be still and just notice what's going on around you. If you can focus on a clock ticking or on taking long, slow breaths, or just really focus on a sound that's going on outside you, this will help. You want to keep yourself grounded. You want to be in the moment. Remind yourself that you are just experiencing a flashback. I know, much easier said than done. But it's a good tip to remember if this happens.

Intrusive Thoughts

Managing the thoughts and feelings associated with the affair can be an enormous task. You might feel as though your feelings, the questions, and memories are always right there in the forefront of your mind, affecting your work, family, and social life. This is a normal response, but you can regain some control over when you let yourself pay attention to the thoughts and feelings.

Managing Thoughts so They Don't Manage You

If you're starting to have distressing thoughts, images, or memories at inconvenient times, I want you to practice saying to yourself, "I'm going to deal with this thought later. I'm going to think about this later." So how is this done?

One tactic is to set aside, every day, a time to worry. I call this, "worry time". Actually schedule a time that you will allow yourself to be anxious and to focus on what happened. At this set-aside time, think about the images and thoughts from the affair that bombard you. Now, I know that some people might see this as crazy, and that's okay with me. The point is, it really does work. You could do it at night, after you come home from work, or maybe at lunchtime. You might need a "worry time" at lunch break because your thoughts are flying all morning when you're at work. So stop and think. This doesn't mean you're going to be calm during this exercise, nor does it mean you aren't going to cry, but I want you to give yourself that time so your body won't find it as necessary to remind you of things and bring them to your attention at less convenient times.

Along with any anxiety, you may also experience some depression. This, too, is a normal response. If you are depressed, you may find that you feel sad or tired, don't want to engage in many of the activities you used to enjoy, don't sleep well, or cry a lot. One part of depression that many people don't realize is that they may experience it as anger and irritability rather than as sadness and crying. Don't overlook this possibility. Depression has many faces.

Professional Help and Medication
If you find that your emotional state is becoming so distressed that you have trouble functioning normally, consult a

professional for treatment or for a medication evaluation. The more positive support you enlist, the better!

Whom to Tell

When you find out that you've been cheated on, it's important to think about *whom* you are going to tell. A lot of people don't know where to go. You don't know whether you should just talk to the priest, rabbi, or pastor; go to a therapist; tell your best friend; tell a couple of people; or just shout it from the bloody rooftops! You will find that the affair consumes your thoughts, and you might find yourself talking about it more often—and maybe to more people—than you are even aware of.

You might find yourself at the grocery store checkout counter, and when the cashier says, "How are you?" you have the urge to say, "Oh, let me tell you how I am: I'm *awful*. My husband has cheated on me, and now my whole life is a mess." I don't suggest that you give in to this urge, but I do want you to know that you are normal if it crosses your mind.

You are consumed with thoughts of the betrayal. You may want to tell everyone: mother, father, aunt, sister, brother, neighbor, mailman, your kids' school bus driver, and all your betrayer's friends. (Now, that last one might give you the satisfaction of revenge, but I don't advise it.) When you find yourself ordering your third milkshake this week, you may want to tell the cashier, "Yes, I'm here again, and let me tell you why: my husband cheated on me, and the only thing that makes me feel happy right now is this frozen treat." All normal.

When you find out that you've been cheated on, it's important to think about whom you're going to tell. Many people don't know where to turn. You don't know whether to tell everyone or no one. My suggestion is to pick one or two people you really trust, who you know can keep things confidential, and let them be your sounding board. Let them guide you, direct you, support you, comfort you, and encourage you. But keep the number of people you tell limited so that you have less distraction, fewer opinions, fewer people who know the lurid details of what your partner did. If you choose to stay with him, the fewer people who know about what happened, the better.

Enlist a "crying crew."

Don't be afraid to let those few people you have chosen to tell about it support you. I like to use the term "crying crew." This is your inner ring of people who are there to wipe your tears, hear your pain, and offer help. These are the people you will talk about the same heartbreaking details with and pose the same unanswered questions to, over and over again. Don't buy into the belief that they are going to get sick of you talking about the affair. For many of us, talking is how we process our feelings. Maybe you've heard the saying: "Let me hear what I say, so I'll know how I feel." Don't feel ashamed about how many times you need to go to them for support.

Let your "crying crew" know what you need from them, and tell them it can change by the day. Some days, you just need them to listen and hold you and let you fall apart and be a mess. Other days, you may need advice. Warn them, though, that you may not take the advice they give, and tell them to not be offended. You are even likely to turn around and do the very opposite of what they say.

Ask them to try to stop you from doing stupid, impulsive things like keying the car of the "other woman" or throwing all your partner's clothes and valuables out on the street for anyone to take. Your "crying crew" will be your anchor during this storm.

Talkin' Trash

As a way of dealing with the pain, you may choose to berate your betrayer to others. You want everybody else to be as angry with him as you are. I must caution you to think about it carefully before you embark down this vengeful path. You see, if you end up staying with your betrayer, and you have spoken negatively about him to those who are closest to you, they might feel protective toward you and not exactly roll out the welcome mat when you decide to keep him in your life. They're going to be angry with the guy who hurt someone they love. They might have a hard time accepting him back into their lives, let alone accepting that *you* are taking him back into yours. You really want to be selective about whom you tell. That way, fewer people are going to resist you if you decide to make a go of it with your partner.

Another thing to consider when deciding whom to tell is that people who hear about how you were betrayed are going to form opinions. They'll likely want to give advice. It's great to have that support, and it's great to have people just listen to you and comfort you, but advice can be very confusing. For one thing, the advice of others is not often very objective, because they're too close. They care for and love you and are invested in your life. They're going to give advice that *they* think is right. And the more people you have advising you, the more confusing it gets for you.

I want you to imagine something. Four months after the affair, you find that you're considering staying in the relationship. Then your closest friend says to you, "Don't you *dare* go back to him! You know the saying, 'once a cheater, always a cheater.' Cut that relationship off and move on." It's going to be hard not to hear that playing in the background as you try to make a decision.

It feels good to tell everyone what happened . . . or does it?

The other thing you should know is that the more you talk about the situation, the more that you retell the story of betrayal, the more it actually *retraumatizes* you. It brings you through that entire event all over again. It's exhausting. It's depressing. It's anxiety provoking, and it really keeps you in that horrible cycle of being traumatized.

You've probably seen this play out in your life before when you tell a story about something that hurt you, and you retell it and retell it and retell it. It actually affects you emotionally. You can be feeling fine and then you tell somebody a story about something that makes you mad, and how do you feel at the end of that story? That's right: you're mad. So you completely changed your mood for the worse just by telling a story. So you may want to think about how emotionally destabilizing it can be for you to continue retelling over and over again the story about what has happened.

Don't rewrite history.

You may find yourself obsessing, questioning the genuineness and reality of your relationship in the first place. It's really normal to go back over the entire time of your relationship and wonder what, if any of it, was real. In my office, I often hear some version of this: "You know what? It was all a sham. None of this was real. They probably haven't been faithful since day one." I caution you not to do that. My clients know that I encourage them NOT to rewrite history. Don't throw the baby out with the bathwater. Just because you've been cheated on doesn't mean that the whole relationship was a farce. Do not taint the memories of your relationship going all the way back to day one, with an affair that went on for only a tiny fraction of that time. I want you to let those memories stay just the way they are. Don't rewrite history in the dark language of the time frame when you were being cheated on.

You ARE absolutely allowed to sit there and say, "I cannot believe that he said he loved me, then slept with somebody else that very night!" Yes, you are definitely allowed to say that. You know, without a shadow of doubt, about some very specific events and times. That is *not* rewriting history.

You may find yourself trying to gather information all the time. In piecing together details, you feel a sense of control or that you are doing something to make sense of the whole thing. You might find yourself caught up in all the fact checking only to wonder why, because "none of it matters now." Don't worry. This, too, is perfectly normal. You'll tell yourself to stop and then find yourself doing it all over again. Normal. Your mind races, checking on things, going back through time and wondering, "*Oh, my Gosh! Was he really going here when he said he was going there?*" That's okay. That's normal.

Grieving

His Grief

Yup, he has to grieve, too. If your partner has left his lover to work it out with you, he's probably grieving. As mad as it might get you to hear this, you need to know that yes, a betrayer will grieve the loss of the lover. I know, I know, this is just salt in the wound. But bear with me on this. They've gone through an intense time together when they've been emotionally and sexually charged. To let this go is not as easy as just saying, "I'm done." In essence, he has been ripped away from a relationship that brought him joy and made him feel alive again.

Bearing this in mind, your partner may not seem his usual self for a while. He's going to miss his lover. Going forward, try to understand and expect this change. Yes, it is unfair that you even have to give a thought to being sensitive to his grieving. It hits a nerve, I'm sure. But don't assume that his having to grieve means that he doesn't want to work on the relationship with you. This is a normal emotional reaction for the betrayer; it really has no bearing on his feelings toward you.

But once this grieving process is over, your partner then needs to be intentional about repairing the relationship with you. Once you have allowed time for him to grieve the loss of his lover, you would be wise to take a look at what kinds of decisions he is making that indicate whether he's even interested in repairing the relationship with you.

Is he trying his best to talk with you? To engage with you again? To do all the things that couples *should* be doing and that you did when you first got together? I really want you to take a look at this. Sometimes, people will grieve the loss of a lover or *seem* to be trying to let it go, but in their mind they really haven't decided whom they really want to be with. It's not crazy to inquire where he is in this process of grieving. Knowledge is power, and knowing what's going on will empower you to make the right decisions going forward.

Your Grief

Right up until that last moment before you found out you were being betrayed, you had this idea of what your life was going to be like going forward. Not one part of that dream had an affair as part of the storyline. Not one part of that dream had you betrayed. And going forward, every step might now feel tainted.

It doesn't have to stay this way forever, but right now EVERYTHING is tainted with the fact that you have been betrayed. So in a way, this is a death—that is, the death of a dream you had. In light of this, it may comfort you to see that as awful as it is, you are progressing through normal, predictable stages of grief as identified by Dr. Elisabeth Kübler-Ross. We often find comfort in predictability, so the following list may be comforting to you.

Denial. One of the first emotions you experience when you find out that yes, you have been cheated on, or when you find signs of it but don't follow up to get confirmation, is denial. You think, "This is not real. This is not actually happening". It's very difficult to accept and own the fact that this has happened. So it's okay that you go through this period of believing against the proof and the odds that you have been betrayed—of not wanting to deal with the betrayal by accepting its reality. It's so much easier to think, "Well, things don't have to change if I don't believe that the affair actually happened."

It's normal that you looked the other way. You hesitated to follow up on the signs. You kept hoping you would be given a good reason why it all happened. When your friends were trying to get you to see through the lies, you still didn't believe it. Again, that's normal.

Anger. Once you allow yourself to acknowledge the inevitable truth, you may find yourself filled with anger. You want to go up to your partner and yell at him and call him all sorts of names. Normal, normal, normal. You have thoughts of throwing clothes out of windows, calling his lover, kicking him out, telling the world that he's a complete louse.

The only thing I'm going to address about this phase is how you *deal* with the anger. Be careful how you respond. Don't do anything you're going to regret. For one, don't get physical. Do not be aggressive. Of course you want to try to stay calm, try to stay in charge of your emotions as much as possible, but you are definitely allowed to be angry, too.

You see, a lot of anger comes from fear. When I'm working with people and they tell me about the things they're angry about, I say to them, "But what are you're really *afraid of*?" The question catches them off guard, but they usually can come up with an answer. Anger grows out of fear.

So what are you afraid of? Fill in the blank, "I am fearful of _____." Look at all the possible fears you may or may not be aware of:

- Will this happen again?
- Maybe I won't ever trust again
- I'm never going to stop hurting.
- I'm not good enough.

You also may fear that your future will not be what you thought it was going to be—and, without your partner, never can be. So many fears come up when you find out you've been cheated on.

- Will I be loved again?
- Will this relationship ever come back?
- Will I be able to make it on my own if I leave?

"He said he loved me!" And that is what makes you angriest.

Bargaining. In this phase, you may deal with some feelings of regret. You go back in time and question, "Well, what if I had looked better?" "What if I had lost those twenty pounds?" "What if he hadn't taken that job?" "Why did I fight so much?"

You go back in time and think that all this could have been controlled. Somehow, something you did contributed to this situation. You may try to rewrite history, imagining some things differently. If you try to take full responsibility while making excuses for your betrayer, I want to caution you: don't buy into the lies—his or yours.

You can go on and on rattling off all the things you believe you had control over that, had you addressed them, would have prevented the affair. My point is this: don't search for explanations of how *you* are responsible for this. Don't own that. I'm not saying there was nothing in the relationship that you could have addressed and that may possibly have made the relationship more vulnerable to the affair, but you are not to take the rap for why your partner cheated. He had a choice. You weren't there. You didn't make that choice for him. He made the choice to cheat on you.

Depression. Kubler- Ross lists depression as stage four in the grief cycle. We have already covered this topic so I won't go into further detail.

Acceptance. Finally, you come to the phase of acceptance. It is at this point you can say that both infidelity and the resultant pain are a fact of your life. You choose to move forward, rebuilding your life while integrating the meaning of the betrayal into your future.

As you go through these phases, realize that they are not linear. By this, I mean, you don't jump from the anger phase to the bargaining phase and then to the acceptance phase. It's not as if you complete one phase and then get to check it off. Rather, you'll go in and out and back and forth from one phase to another. You might be depressed for a while and then angry; then you might want to rewrite history and then you accept it—right before you go back to being angry again. These stages can overlap, and you can revisit each of them. It is overall that you will see a slow progression through these emotional phases, leading up to the point of acceptance.

DO NOT MAKE A DECISION!

The next thing I'm going to tell you is to hold off on deciding whether to stay in this relationship. You are living the future right now. All of what you are going through is part of it. The process of dealing with the infidelity will *eventually* bring you to a place of decision. But for now, hold off on trying to decide whether to stay or go.

It's natural that the first thing you want to do is decide whether you should stay with him or leave. You really are in no place to make a decision of this gravity right now. Your emotions are too inconsistent. You haven't had time to decide whether you can trust or forgive. And you haven't given it time to see whether your betrayer is willing to rebuild your relationship— or indeed whether he even wants to. It can take one to two years to know fully whether you can stay in a relationship that you've been betrayed in. So this should tell you that the decision-making process should take some time, and that's okay. Resist the urge to come up with an immediate decision just so you'll have an answer for either yourself or others.

I applaud you for not rushing to a decision, for being willing to let things unfold, and for trying to be comfortable in the waiting. When it comes to decision making, I always encourage my clients to make any decision in such a way that when you look back in time and evaluate *how you arrived* at that decision, you have no regrets.

What-If Thinking

One big contributor to depression that I often come across in my office is what I like to call "what-if thinking." This is that uncomfortable emotional/mental state where you question decisions you have made and how you made them. You go back and forth, wondering whether you did the right thing. You can start to obsess over the decision, to the point of being stuck. Rather than go forward and live out the decisions you made, you continue to evaluate whether you made a good decision. This type of questioning and insecurity can disturb your peace and impede your ability to move ahead.

For example, let's say you were to kick your partner out immediately after discovering the affair. Your belief was that when it comes to fidelity, nobody deserves a second chance. You were angry, hurt, and humiliated. You reacted in the moment.

Now picture yourself three months down the road. You wonder, "What if I had waited to kick him out? Could he have changed?" "Would it have worked out if I had given it a chance?" "What if there were things I did to weaken the relationship"? These are the sort of questions that can keep you stuck. Regret keeps you in the past and makes it hard to live in the present, in peace.

Take your time to make the right decision. There's no rush. Seriously, why on earth would you want to rush this? What could that possibly help? Right now you need to take care of yourself. Decisions can wait.

What do I tell others?

Practice what we mentioned in chapter one. When anyone asks you whether you are going to stay or go, be a broken record.

You might want to use this statement: "I'm putting all decisions on hold and just focusing on taking care of me for now."

And while we're on the topic of what to tell others, I want to remind you that you have permission not to talk at all. I'll say it again: YOU DO NOT HAVE TO TALK AT ALL IF YOU DON'T WANT TO. Remember, it's nobody's business but your own. Too often, we think it would be rude of us not to answer a question. You can respond to anyone by saying, with a smile if you like, "Thanks for asking, but I'd rather discuss something more uplifting, if you don't mind," or words to that effect. The main point, though, is that if you don't feel like discussing the issue every time you are with people, *don't.* Acknowledge their concern and thank them for caring; then suggest another topic. I practice this in session with my clients often. You will feel much less anxiety knowing you can be in charge of where and when you discuss this issue.

—*Exercise*—
Dealing with the Questions of Others

Throughout your personal journey of dealing with the infidelity, there will be people who ask questions. It will be best to prepare yourself to give an answer. Is this necessary? No. Is it reality? Yes.

After the initial revelation of the affair, most people want to know, "Are you going to stay in the relationship?" You are wise not to make any decisions at this point, but I want you to think about a blanket statement that you can give everyone.

Having a ready answer is important because it removes you from a place of anxiety when you are out and about with people. Your initial reaction to the revelation of infidelity is to avoid social situations for this very reason: because you feel as though you must give explanations. When you are prepared with a response, you won't feel tongue-tied when asked for a reply.

I suggest coming up with a sentence or two that states your choice with confidence—not a justification. For example, you might respond to an inquiry about whether you are going to stay with your partner, by saying, "The right thing for me right now is to stay in the relationship." That doesn't open up the door for much further questioning. If people push (which is rude but will happen), you just become a broken record and repeat the statement: "The right thing for me right now is to stay in the relationship." It's vague, doesn't tell your exact plan, and reveals exactly what you *are* doing.

Yes, it will feel weird, but it works. Trust me. Even if you are shaking inside when you say this, it's okay. As I say to my clients, "You fake it till you make it." This is no different. The act of confidence usually precedes the "real deal." After applying this technique a couple of times, you will begin to breeze through the response.

Another Reason a Quick Decision Is No Good

Here's another thing that can happen in relationships where betrayal has occurred: either the betrayed or the betrayer becomes so focused on keeping the relationship intact, they never even consider whether they even *want* the relationship.

In my office, I ask people, "If your partner stays with you and you get past the pain of what's happened, and things go back to exactly the way they were before, do you still want to be in this relationship?" It's interesting to see how many of them have never thought about that. And quite a few admit that the relationship was really not that great in the first place. I encourage you to consider whether you really do want to fight for it and whether you really want it back.

The betrayer also needs to consider this issue. He can get so caught up in proving himself to you that he doesn't really think about why he cheated—or whether he wants to go back to how things were.

No Begging

Whatever you do, don't try to make someone stay by being emotionally manipulative. It just ends up making you feel powerless. I'm talking about the all-too-common dance where a relationship is on the verge of being over until one person begs, pleads, cries, and tugs on the other's heartstrings and they end up staying together—for now. Few things are sadder to see than someone trying to convince their partner to stay when the partner has already decided to move on. If someone doesn't want to be with you, why would you want to be with him? You are worth being wanted. Trust me on this.

So what's next?

As crazy as it sounds, you're going to try doing life again so that it seems something like the life you had before you found out you were betrayed. Yes, everything has changed at this point and you have a lot of thinking to do, emotions to process, and decisions to make. All this will continue, but meanwhile, we will focus on how to begin picking up the pieces and putting your life back together again.

So to review, you have permission to . . .

- cry
- scream
- feel like hurting him (but don't do it)
- leave for a bit
- kick him out
- tell those who love you about the infidelity
- go to work
- stay home from work
- eat junk food
- stay on the couch
- run five miles
- start a new project
- finish an old project
- go on a trip
- hide in bed
- do nothing

In short, you have permission to be a mess. It's not glamorous, but you are ever so much more than that!

— Ask Yourself —

What's Normal?

1. What things might you need to give up for a while to make getting through each day easier as you process the shock of the betrayal?

2. Whom can you ask to hold you accountable but not let you isolate yourself completely while you allow for a "time-out"?

3. What is the most prominent emotion you are experiencing? Anger? Sadness? Fear? Embarrassment?

4. Are you allowing yourself to *feel* these feelings?

Anxiety, Depression, and PTSD

1. Have you had flashbacks? Of what images or scenes? Where were you when the flashbacks occurred?

2. Write down your "worry time" plan here:

Whom to Tell

1. Write down your list of who you think is safe to tell about the betrayal, and why.

2. Are you retraumatizing yourself by retelling your story?

Rewriting History

1. Have you tried to rewrite some of the events and memories from your relationship history?

2. If so, take a good look at what you are rewriting. Is it valid that you question this time in your relationship history?

Grief

1. Has your partner been grieving?

2. Can you allow him the space to do this?

3. Do you believe the lie that his grief over the affair means he doesn't love you?

4. What signs did you ignore? Who tried to let you know? What kept you from checking into the signs?

5. What is the biggest fear that is making you angry? Is it a justified fear? What is the likelihood of that fear coming true?

6. What phase of the grief cycle are you in now?

7. What signs/behaviors tell you that?

8. What phases have you gone through?

Judging the Relationship

1. Do you want the relationship back as it was? Have you evaluated it from a distance, both the good and the bad?

2. Do you think the relationship can improve if you get past the affair?

3. If your partner does not want to take you back, can you accept that?

4. Why is it, or will it be, hard for you to accept that he wants to move on?

5. Is staying in a relationship where you are not treasured a relationship pattern for you?

6. What will keep you from letting go?

7. What will help you let go and move on?

Chapter 4

———

"You Want Me to *What*?"

A relationship can survive infidelity. Indeed, it can actually be *better* after an affair. It's in moving from the point of discovery to decision that you learn to rework and explore the dynamics of the relationship. Assuming that both you and your partner are choosing to move in the direction of saving the relationship, there will have to be some changes made.

While you're waiting to make that decision, trust is the point of focus for you. For you to let yourself be present, comfortable, and vulnerable in the relationship, your trust must be rebuilt. And for that to happen, you will need to establish some guidelines.

New Rules

There's a saying: "You give someone your trust the first time; the second time, they have to earn it." Like it or not, your partner must earn back your trust.

At this point, your partner has lost the privilege of privacy. Some people are going to take issue with me when I say this. I have had some professionals say to the betrayer that everybody deserves privacy regardless of what they've done. I don't *completely* disagree with that. Let me explain . . .

Your partner must be willing to be completely transparent with you. He has to agree to give you access to many forms of his communication. For you to feel comfortable, you might have to ask your partner to close out his Facebook account. Maybe for a time, they won't be going out alone socially. Perhaps your partner needs to join a new gym if that's where he met his lover. You may ask to oversee household finances if you realize his betrayal would have been picked up sooner, had you watched credit cards and bank accounts closer. Hear me loud and clear, *"you get to ask for what you need!"*

What might this look like? Everyone has their own personal level of comfort. What creates mistrust and anxiety for one will not be the same for someone else. As the two of you establish new relationship guidelines, few requests are unreasonable, especially in the beginning.

Open-Book Policy

What I'm describing here is an "open-book" policy. This means you have access to all that is going on in your partner's life. In essence, he must be willing (key word: "*willing*") to be transparent with his life. In my office, far too often I see the betrayer get fired up at the mention of this idea. Your partner's resistance should be the tip-off that he is probably doing something he shouldn't. If there is nothing to hide . . . there is *nothing* to hide. When you ask him to take the password off his phone, he should agree. When you say you want to look at his social media pages and view his computer history, it shouldn't be a problem. When you ask him to take most phone calls in your presence, that shouldn't be a problem, either. Your partner should show an overall willingness to do whatever it takes to rebuild trust with you.

Otherwise, if you get a lot of kicking and screaming and comments such as "What about my need for privacy?" before you even get rolling with your requests, that should be a big red flag.

Ending the Affair

I shouldn't have to tell you that your partner has to cut off ALL communication with his lover. If you are trying to rebuild the relationship, this is nonnegotiable. You can't possibly heal when you know that he is still in a relationship. Don't buy into the whole "I need to let her down slowly" crock. I suggest that you both agree on when and how your partner will contact his lover to sever the relationship. You many even want to be present in some way. He doesn't need to coddle his lover; he just needs to say it's over.

A word of caution is in order here: just because your partner agrees to end the relationship with his lover doesn't necessarily mean that things are *over* between the two of them. I say this not to discourage you but to arm you with the knowledge that emotions don't stop the moment contact and communication cease. We certainly hope that your partner is agreeable to ending things with his lover, but be aware that forced decisions can backfire. As hard as it may be, you may have to give your partner some time to decide, on his own, *whom* he wants to be in a relationship with. Ending the relationship is definitely a justifiable request, but with it can come uncertainty about just how genuine your partner's decision to let it go really is.

Ending the Workplace Affair

A fairly common situation is the *office affair.* Many affairs happen between coworkers. I don't think it's out of the question for your partner to switch jobs, but that's just my opinion, popular or not. If this is nonnegotiable and he has to stay at the same workplace, then you need to have some very clear and specific boundaries around what will happen when he interacts with his former lover.

You and your partner need to be very specific about "allowable" communications. Now, this is going to be very difficult for you. It's unfortunate that you have to be put in this situation, but that's the way it is. Unless you're following your partner to work every day, you're going to have to trust him. I know . . . right? Trust: the one thing you really can't do right now. You will have to step out on faith and believe he is going to follow the rules you've set up.

You are going to discuss together the new rules and the boundaries he needs to have with his former lover. The two of you can decide what is appropriate. Is only e-mail communication allowed? Phone meetings? What degree and forms of communication do they need in order to work together? Is he allowed to have personal conversations at lunchtime? Is he even allowed to have lunch together at all? Is he allowed to talk at the water cooler? The two of you need to decide what's appropriate.

Allow me to make a suggestion here. Anything outside the realm of work is off limits. They have already shown you that they cannot draw a strong boundary between working relationships and intimate relationships. The two of you must specifically indicate what that boundary looks like.

How Things Might Turn Out

One of the responses you might get from your partner when you ask him to have an open-book policy with you is that he agrees but asks to go through his phone, e-mail, and social media first and get rid of anything associated with the betrayal. Obviously, your partner will want to erase anything from before the revelation of the betrayal and "start fresh" once the open-book policy is in place.

If you think it would be helpful for your healing, let your partner know that you would like to sit down and go through the erasing process together. Is this going to meet with some resistance? Count on it. Then again, your partner might be a little more amenable to this option than to your going through everything on your own!

Let him know that this is not how things are going to be forever. Remind him that you didn't ask to be in this position in the first place. Yes, it can feel as though you're acting rather parental toward the one who has cheated on you. I'm not a big advocate for parental dynamics in any relationship, but with infidelity, there has to be some accountability for a time.

Once you feel that your partner has begun to earn your trust, you can slowly back off from some of the strict guidelines that were put in place when trust was nonexistent. You can decide how long this needs to go on. Really, the gauge is going to be how *you* feel. For some people, it's just a couple of weeks; for others, it could be a couple of months. This is all with the understanding that if you begin to find some suspicious behavior, the whole process may start all over again.

I was seeing Olivia and Scott in my office. Olivia, an older professional woman who worked as a lawyer, asked for access to her husband's e-mail and phone as part of the plan to rebuild trust. Scott, a handsome man who worked as a mechanic and had a history of broken promises and repeated affairs, balked at this idea from the start, saying that "everybody has a right to privacy." After much hesitation, and threats by Olivia to end the relationship if he couldn't commit to the plan, he agreed. (I'll bet you can guess how well this went.) After six-months of couples therapy, Scott said during our session, "We've been doing this for six months now. Shouldn't this be long enough?"

Typically, I would have agreed, but during those six months, Olivia kept finding incriminating evidence of his continued affairs. Scott didn't understand that it's not the length of time that you're being monitored; it's the consistency over time that you prove yourself trustworthy. Every time you discover that your partner has "slipped up," all the trust goes out the window, and the rebuilding process starts all over again. He has to understand this. Trust is something he has to earn continuously, not just "most of the time." Scott may have thought he had been earning trust for six months, but with each revelation of dishonesty, he was starting back at day one.

I'm not trying to be an extremist here. You are not going to be privy to every one of your partner's phone conversations, nor does this mean that you have the right to go through every one of his e-mails and read *all* of them. I want to be clear in saying that if you are going to be checking your partner's phone, texts, and e-mails, you should decide together which ones you'll be looking at. I don't think you should get to have 100 percent access to every bit of communication your partner has. There is no need for you to be reading work memos, no need for you to be monitoring conversations with friends. Again, you want to agree ahead of time on the types of information you will be looking at. I understand that this may not be a popular idea, but it's necessary.

The open-book policy is no guarantee against your partner's ever cheating again. It's a tool to use that requires effort from your partner. Thus, it signifies your mutual agreement toward the goal of trust. In the end, though, your partner's attitude about the negotiations and policies will really be the telltale sign of commitment.

— Ask Yourself —

1. What do you need from your partner in order to feel that you can start to trust again?

2. Describe your partner's response to this request. What does that response mean to you?

3. How long do you think your partner should have to agree to be transparent with you in order to earn back your trust?

Chapter 5

Back to a Seminormal Life

L ife will never go *completely* back to the way it was, but you'll slowly find your way back to some of the same daily patterns you had before the infidelity. This is a good thing. There is comfort in familiarity and predictability. Getting back to the way things were is necessary as you continue to process through your emotions about the betrayal. You don't have to make the decision whether to stay or go before life can "go back to normal." You should feel a freedom to go on dates again with your partner (or start if you weren't before), be social together, rejoin family activities, and make love. This chapter explores some of the concerns you may have about how to interact with your partner when you are still undecided whether to stay with him.

Some Common Concerns

If I have fun, will he think I've decided to stay?

I don't want you to worry that if you laugh and relax around your partner, it will send the message that you have forgiven, forgotten, and simply moved past the pain of the betrayal. You're not doing that. Just because you can laugh with your partner again doesn't mean that what he did was okay. I want you to cancel out that thought altogether. Give yourself permission to respond as your genuine self. It will be important for you to see if you can relax and enjoy being with your partner again. This is all part of your decision-making process. I urge you, though, don't be afraid to give in to the desire to be close to your partner again. It will be important to take a step back and remember that your relationship is about more than the betrayal. If you focus only on the infidelity, you can quickly lose traction on repairing the relationship, because you are not experiencing each other in all the ways that brought you together in the first place.

It's not uncommon to worry that if you start to act "normal" again, your partner will think you've decided to stay in the relationship. If this is a fear of yours, then have a conversation with your partner and state clearly that you haven't decided yet about the fate of the relationship. Let him know that you aren't trying to lead him on by doing the things you used to do as a couple. Explain that given the major trust issues that are still very much unresolved, you need to experience the relationship fully, in light of what has happened, to really know whether you can still be happy going forward. Aside from that conversation, give yourself permission to be fully present in the relationship.

I just can't relax with him anymore.

It may just be too difficult to relax with your partner—to let go of the images and the pain. You may find yourself continually checking to see if what your partner tells you is really the truth. You feel anxious all the time and see no decrease in your anxiety with the passing of time. You may find that six months down the road, all the memories, images, and hurt are just as fresh in your mind now as on the day you found out. Unfortunately, you can't even know that until you're six months down the road. You want to observe how you respond and attend to the signals your body and mind are sending you. It could be that you *won't* be able to move beyond the betrayal and stay with your partner.

How will I know I'm starting to move past the pain?

In the initial days, weeks, and months after the betrayal comes to light, you will want to reflect on your behavior. Can you have sex again and without bad images filling up your mind? Can you drive down the street, past the bar where your partner met his lover, and not feel the hurt and anger as intensely as in the beginning? Do you constantly question whether your partner is genuine in his communication? That is, do you doubt his expressions of love toward you?

Are you micromanaging your environment by cutting out any and all triggers that bring the affair to mind? For example, have you gotten rid of the couch that your partner and his lover kissed passionately on? Do you turn the radio off every time you hear the style of music they both enjoyed? Evaluate your responses from day to day. The hope is that you can get through the normal parts of your life again without the thoughts of betrayal interfering with *everything* you do.

A Caution against Becoming a Victim

One thing that can happen when you've been betrayed is that your identity starts to get wrapped up in the fact that you are a victim of infidelity. The hurt of the betrayal becomes the overriding theme in your life.

If you adopt this pattern of thinking, you begin to look at everything through the "victim" lens. Whatever happens to go wrong in your life, you somehow connect it back to the betrayal. The result of this kind of thinking is that you might start to direct all your anger and frustration at your partner and, perhaps unknowingly, operate under the belief that he needs to pay you penance.

What might it look like if you have fallen prey to this victim mentality? It may be that not a day goes by that you don't remind your partner of what he did to hurt you. Or maybe you have the expectation that your partner should treat you better than ever—"kiss your butt," in less refined language. What you may not realize is that just because your partner is not talking about the betrayal does not mean that he is any less mindful of what he did. It's possible that he thinks about it as much as you do. But it isn't a comfortable topic for him, so it's likely you will have no idea how often these thoughts run through his mind. Your continued need to make him feel guilty for what has happened may be a sign that you've identified with being a victim.

If you have chosen to move forward, there should be a noticeable shift from being a victim to being an overcomer. I like to use that word: "overcomer." It encapsulates all I could ever hope for you at this point in the healing. Overcomers don't deny the horrible truth that has become their reality, but they don't let it keep them down, either. They choose to move past the painful event and come out stronger on the other side. They have a conscious mind-set to forge ahead and be strong.

It may be that you are not even aware that you're stuck in the victim mentality. You might want to ask those closest to you (and, if you're brave enough, ask your partner as well) whether you are identifying with this debilitating thinking. If you don't make a conscious point to stop identifying with this type of thinking, you could remain stuck indefinitely at this stage in the journey.

As tough as things have been for you, if you relate to your partner in this unhealthy way, it will most likely result in his becoming resentful and even unsure whether *he* wants to stay in the relationship. He may feel, understandably, that if payback is all you want, being together just isn't worth it. After all, what kind of a life is it for him if he's constantly going to have to wear that scarlet letter? I have seen this play out in my office. The betrayer can grovel only for so long before he despairs of ever being happy in the relationship again. And so he decides just to move on, even if reconciliation is what he had initially hoped for.

What if he's staying with me just because he "has to"?

Often, the one who has been betrayed doesn't trust the partner's attempts at restoring the relationship. You question whether your partner really does want to be with you. How will you know?

What types of things should you be noticing while you're in this "holding pattern"? Right now you are most likely "doing life" with no decision made about the future of the relationship. How do you know if your partner really wants to make things better? Do you know if he's staying because he wants to or just because "it's the right thing to do"? This is a legitimate concern. I have had clients tell me that they think their partner is just pretending to want to make things work, when he is really just trying to buy time to figure out the best exit plan. Or, worse, your partner's lover is the one who ended the relationship, making it hard for you to be certain he's staying with you for the right reasons. Let's explore what to watch for as you move forward and address some of these fears.

The Tricky Part of Trust (the Second Time Around)

You are being asked to trust the behavior and words of someone who has proved untrustworthy. How do you handle this fear you have of being lied to again? How can you move forward when you are constantly afraid of being blindsided not once but *twice*? Three words: *do it scared*.

"Do it scared."

I use this term often with my clients. I tell them we can get through anything together, but they first need to accept the fact that they are going to have to do many things I ask of them while feeling scared. You can't wait until you feel 100 percent ready to move forward. I'm telling you up front that it's going to feel awful. There will be no guarantees. You are going to feel anxious. You'll feel sick at your stomach some days. Tears will abound. Questions will consume you. The temptation will loom to throw in the towel and turn back. This is what it looks like when you "do it scared." I will reiterate my belief that if you go into something with realistic expectations about how bad things might turn out, anything less than your worst-case scenario doesn't seem so bad. I believe in envisioning the worst so that you are better prepared to deal with it if it should become reality.

There are things to look for as you try your best to believe and trust your partner. Observe. Does he seem genuinely interested in your healing? Does he ask how you're doing? If so, this is a positive sign that he acknowledges his part in your pain and is taking responsibility for it. Does your partner genuinely feel guilt for what he did? Does he have remorse? Is it easy for him to say, "I'm sorry"? Or does he seem to be choking on these words? Is he patient with you as you heal? Does he show a willingness to do the things you ask of him? Overall, do you see him trying to invest in you and the relationship? Or has he simply decided that he can't be with his lover, and that's about as far as it goes?

If your partner stays with you out of obligation and guilt, what kind of future is that? You want to see your partner working actively to make your relationship better. If he's just going through the motions, it's going to be a challenge for you to believe that he won't stray again.

But he's all I've ever known.

When infidelity affects a relationship with a long history, it seems especially difficult for the one betrayed to imagine life with anyone else, regardless of the pain of the betrayal. So you are tempted to stay in the relationship out of fear of the unknown.

Jolene had been married almost thirty years when her husband cheated. At first, she didn't care—she was ready to forgive almost immediately. All she wanted was to stay with her husband and get back to the security of that relationship. For her, glossing over the betrayal was easier than imagining life without him or with another person. Along with being fearful of the unknown, this sweet woman had bought into a self-imposed rule that "I will love only once." Week after week, she would come into my office and report that she was still waiting for her husband to "make a decision." Each week, she would come back more depressed and hopeless than ever, so I encouraged her to find something new and exciting to add to her life—a positive distraction from the intense pain and hurt. I wanted her to stop keeping her life on hold.

As she gave herself permission to enjoy life and explore new interests instead of just waiting for the verdict, an interesting thing happened: she met someone. She took a class to enrich her own life and, in the process, met a man and found true friendship. Her eyes opened up to the realization that she was not having her needs met in her marriage even before the betrayal ever happened. She realized that even if her husband chose to stay with her, she didn't want things back the way they were—she wanted them better or not at all. Experiencing life in a new way removed the fear of the unknown and opened up possibilities she hadn't seen before.

The previous story highlights two important points to consider when you are trying to get back to life as you knew it:

1. Don't lose sight of who you are outside the infidelity.
2. Take the time to consider how healthy your relationship was before he cheated.

I often encourage my clients to get involved in something that enhances their life "in the waiting." As I said before, it's far too easy to get so focused on the infidelity that you forget there is more to you and your own life than just that. Working through infidelity is exhausting. It depletes you emotionally and physically. This makes it that much more important for you to consider how you will take care of yourself. How will you hold on to your identity in all this? What is going to give you strength, peace, and joy while you're waiting? As painful and tiring as it is to work through betrayal, don't ignore your friends, hobbies, and health. Stay grounded in your identity. You are more than the infidelity!

Giving the Relationship an Honest Evaluation

How healthy was your relationship before the infidelity? This question gets overlooked far too easily. The cheating and lying become the overriding concern, to the exclusion of looking at the aspects of the relationship that may have contributed to the infidelity in the first place. It's far too easy to get caught up in the crisis of the affair and focus on the pieces of the relationship that need to be repaired as a *result* of the betrayal. The danger here is that you overlook the parts that were already broken before the affair ever happened.

This is the focus of the next chapter: evaluating the overall health of your relationship and looking at how and why the affair happened. Once you have dealt with these issues, you begin to move closer to that place of decision—a place that can feel very far away from where you're standing right now.

1. How would you describe your interactions with your partner? Guarded? Open?
2. Not *will you* but *can you* relax in the relationship at this point?

3. Overall, do you think you are moving forward in the process of restoring the relationship? Or are you stuck?

4. Is it possible that you might be (however subtly) reminding your partner about his transgressions as a way to feel safe and in control?

5. Do you act as if your partner owed you something?

6. Are you a victim or an overcomer?

7. Does your partner's behavior suggest that he truly desires to be in a relationship with you?

8. Do you have within you the hope that you can be happy either with or without your partner?

9. Will fear of the unknown be a factor in your choice to stay in the relationship?

10. Are you continuing to participate in all the parts of your life that make it balanced: hobbies, exercise, spiritual activities, and keeping up with friends?

11. Do you feel that your relationship was a healthy one before the betrayal?

Chapter 6

"How Could You!"

It's tough being blindsided by the news of the affair. You probably thought your relationship was doing okay. You believed that everything was normal. Of course there were good days and bad days, but overall, things were good. Your belief was that your partner would never cheat on you. If he were "a cheater," you would never have entered into a relationship with him, right?

So how do you spot a guy who might cheat?

Who cheats?

Peggy Vaughan, author of *The Monogamy Myth*, says that 60 percent of men and 40 percent of women cheat. Since those 60 percent of men and 40 percent of women are not necessarily married to each other, this means that just over three-quarters of all marriages will experience betrayal[4].

When you find out about an affair, please don't make the mistake of thinking that the relationship has gone horribly wrong and you were naive to have missed it. While it is true that people who say their relationship is "not too happy" are four times as likely to engage in infidelity,[5] it is not uncommon for cheaters to report that they are satisfied with their relationship. (I know: seems strange, doesn't it?)

There is no one factor that leads to infidelity, and there is no one type of person who has an affair. I find myself saying this a lot to my clients: *There is no type!*

I'd be rich if I had a dollar for every time a woman, in shock and denial at the realization that she's being cheated on, says one or more of the following:

> *"But he's not like that!"*
> *"He hates people who cheat on their wives."*
> *"He's not a liar."*
> *"His own father cheated, and he hates that."*

The following are factors that may increase the odds that your partner will cheat. A caveat is important here, though: please don't allow this list to plant fear in you or become a source for you to create a string of "if, then" statements. For example, "*if* your partner has been divorced, *then* he will cheat." This list is simply a guide to help you understand factors that *may* have contributed to your experience of infidelity.

- *Divorce.* Men and women who are divorced are twice as likely to be unfaithful.[6]
- *Getting married at a young age.* Someone who married at 16 years of age is four times as likely to cheat as someone who married at 23 or older.[7]
- *Income.* People who earn $75,000 or more per year are 1.5 times as likely to have an affair as those earning $30,000 a year.[8]
- *Education.* People with the most and least education are more likely to cheat. This refers to those with less than an eighth-grade education, or an education beyond a master's degree.[9]
- *Lack of religious beliefs.* People who never attend religious services are 2.5 times as likely to cheat as those who attend services more than once a week.[10]

The Importance of Opportunity

Even if your partner meets the criteria for some of the above-listed variables, what ultimately leads to an affair is the alignment of several different variables that create just the right atmosphere for infidelity to erupt—a "perfect storm." In other words, all the unforeseen variables that could increase the odds of an affair happening all line up at the same time, giving the person an opportunity to choose to cheat. Each situation is unique, and the variables necessary to make the choice will vary from person to person. I'll use a classic example to clarify:

Don's wife left for a business trip after yet another heated argument about their finances. That same day, after working later than normal at the office, Don and his charming female coworker decided to get dinner together. They had a drink or two, and one thing led to another. (You can fill in the rest of the story.)

I'm guessing that neither Don nor his coworker went out seeking an affair. Rather, the "perfect storm" was created when all the above variables came together: argument, wife out of town, working late, alcohol, charming coworker. If any of those variables were to change, the likelihood of the affair happening would decrease.

When considering infidelity, it's important to remember *opportunity*. When a relationship is left neglected and vulnerable and an opportunity to get a need met arises outside that relationship, the likelihood of someone cheating goes up. Consider this example:

Jill and Brian had been discussing marriage for quite some time. Jill thought that after dating for eight years, Brian was finally going to propose. When Valentine's Day (the day she had hinted at, hoping to get a proposal) came and went, she was heartbroken. The next weekend, when she went "out with the girls," she bumped into an old flame at a bar. After one too many drinks, she found herself in bed with him the next morning.

When Jill came to me for therapy, she was distraught. She had never intended to cheat on Brian. She was appalled at her own behavior. How could she do that to someone she loved so deeply? Without letting herself off the hook for cheating, but taking full responsibility for her choice, Jill eventually realized that her hurt and disappointment—along with poor judgment from drinking, and the open arms of someone who made her feel desirable when she was feeling rejected—all contributed to her choosing to cheat. Again, the perfect storm of opportunity combined with vulnerability of the relationship led to unexpected infidelity.

So why do affairs happen?

I need to state here that just because someone doesn't believe in cheating has no bearing on whether they will cheat. Ninety percent of people say they think cheating is wrong[11], yet 60 percent of men and 40 percent of women do it. So how does this make sense? I find that it serves as confirmation that most affairs are not planned. With that said, I am going to list some of the most common factors that increase the possibility of an infidelity.

The Friend-Turned-Lover Affair

Often, an affair happens when what began as a friendship turns into something more. Also, it's not uncommon that the two people involved in an affair are members of two couples who spend a lot of time together. Let's consider the dynamics here.

As couples, the four of you go out often, spend a lot of time together, laugh together, have common interests, and may even learn some intimate details of each other's lives. With everyone being married/committed, there's something akin to a false sense of security in this type of situation. It's a safe environment where you can examine another person. All parties involved are experienced in a good light. If the right opportunity comes along, an affair can blossom quite easily.

This is such a slow process, nobody really even seems to notice at first. Of course, hindsight is always 20/20. Once the affair comes to light, you can look back and watch the unfolding of events that led to it. More than once, I have sat with a woman who couldn't believe it was her best friend that her husband ended up betraying her with.

This is where I want to pause for a moment and comment on the woman who is "too trusting." I hear these words spoken in pain far too often from my clients who have been cheated on:

"It was like I was almost pushing my husband into my friend's arms."

Now, I'm not saying you should live feeling insecure or fearful that your partner will want to sleep with every friend you have. But don't forget that human vulnerability can take over. I am a firm believer that you should *never* get so comfortable in your relationship that you think an affair is an impossibility. The risk always exists. I received this advice when I was having premarital counseling for my own marriage, and I see the importance of these words in my office every day. The reason no relationship is immune is because most people don't *intend* to have an affair, or even think it's going to happen in their relationship. Again, I am not suggesting that you not trust your partner, but you need to be realistic about how easily an affair can start, so that you are constantly aware of the importance of protecting a relationship.

The Workplace Affair

The most common affair is the workplace affair. It's a perfect opportunity for a friendship or professional partnership to slip into something more intimate without either person even really noticing. Coworkers are talking throughout the day, having lunch in the cafeteria together, meeting at the water cooler, maybe even commuting together. Obviously, they're going to share details of their lives. The danger starts when, over time, the conversations deepen into more intimate details that shouldn't be shared. Discussions about frustrations at home, sharing details of fights with your partner, maybe even jokingly discussing behavior in the bedroom—any of these things creates a deepened relationship.

Before long, you begin to experience excitement at the thought of seeing your coworker and sharing the details of your life—more so than with your own partner. You give more mental energy and thought to your interactions with your coworker rather than with your actual partner. Before long, if the feeling is mutual and opportunity presents itself, an affair is under way.

It's normal to be attracted.

I want to clarify something here. It's not noticing or being attracted to another person that is the problem. It's when you *act* on that attraction. Denying that you can feel attraction to someone besides your partner can cause problems for both you and your partner.

For example, I've had men and women fight in my office about this very issue. A woman will share concerns about her partner's "noticing" another attractive female. The man who has "taken notice" will try to deny it, usually insulting the intelligence of his partner with a response such as this:

"I don't notice anyone but you, honey."

"I didn't even see the person you're talking about."

"All other girls are ugly to me."(Yeah, right.)

Before things get too heated between the partners, I will usually jump in and challenge this denial of attraction by confirming the obvious:

"With human attraction, we all know there is no switch that goes to 'off' the minute we fall in love and commit to a relationship. We don't just suddenly stop noticing beauty or responding physically to it. There is nothing wrong with appreciating a beautiful person; we just can't act on those feelings"

(And because I am the professional saying this, somehow the idea is now okay with everyone.)

Media Opportunities, Texting, Apps, and Other Forms of Digital Communication

All the various technologies available to us that help us communicate without face-to-face interaction have opened up the door for many affairs: Facebook, Internet chat rooms, phone apps that keep conversations hidden, and the multiplicity of pornography sites, to name just a few. These forms of electronic contact might begin online but can easily be continued in person. With twenty-four-hour access, it's easy to find someone who is "available" online when your partner isn't around to meet your emotional or sexual needs.

There is something about being behind a "screen" (computer, phone, or tablet) that creates a sense of anonymity. Suddenly, you feel free to say things you might not be comfortable saying when you're sitting right next to someone. You might be more open to talking about sex and your emotions. You feel free to experiment with a different persona in a safe way—maybe show a side of you that you are not as confident about displaying in normal circumstances.

We see this sort of behavior every day. How often do you yourself share a text or e-mail in which you have written what you wouldn't say in person? We feel a level of safety in the written or typed word that isn't there in face-to-face interactions. Compared to years ago, when communication with a lover could happen only in person or by phone (both of which required much tedious planning to keep secret), today you can have an intimate relationship with someone who is not your partner and stay in almost constant communication with them while easily keeping it secret.

Rekindling the Old Flame

The social media known as Facebook has contributed to another common type of affair: reconnecting with an old flame. It's easy to romanticize how this relationship used to be, even if it wasn't actually so wonderful. People tend to remember the good and forget the bad while rekindling the relationship. Put on the rose-tinted glasses, add a little curiosity, and throw in the added comfort and familiarity that these two people share, and you quickly have the ingredients for an affair.

Feeling Taken for Granted

It happens—two people stay in a relationship for a while, and one begins to take the other for granted. If this happens and somebody on the outside starts to give your partner the attention they need, it may make them desire more interaction with that person. Your partner begins to think about that person more often and maybe even seeks to impress them. Your partner will begin to experience excitement at the thought of being with that person again. This becomes risky territory because people become vulnerable to acting on their feelings. At minimum, this becomes an emotional affair.

With time, it is not uncommon for a relationship to fall into neglect. "Neglect" means that you and your partner are not connecting, spending time together, and being interested in each other's lives. This opens up the door for someone else to come along and meet those needs.

In another scenario, the partner who feels neglected may seek out an affair with the intention of being found out. He wants you to discover the affair, so that you will be reminded that he is desirable to other people. He hopes you will then pay him more attention to prevent him from cheating again (definitely not a great plan).

The Troubled Relationship

Some people have affairs because the relationship is in trouble and they want to escape. The increase in tension and conflict can contribute to cheating. An affair has all the appealing elements that seem to be missing.

When you are having an affair, the experience is unrealistic and takes place in a fantasy bubble. You feel the thrill of passion and secrecy. You have no daily stresses to deal with. The mundane details of life that lead people to fight don't exist. Not to mention the adrenaline rush of sneaking around and getting the complete attention of another person. This is an easy distraction from the reality of a bad relationship. A conflicted relationship can't stand up to the positive feelings attached to the affair or the idealized lover.

It isn't a matter of whether he still loves you.
Cheating doesn't mean your partner doesn't love you. I know, these are hard words to swallow, and most people get angry when they hear them. But they are true. Many people cheat but still profess their love for their partner. When somebody chooses to cheat, they typically are being selfish and not thinking about the other person's feelings. In that moment, it's all about him and what he needs and what he wants. He can be in love with you and still make the awful choice to get his needs met outside your relationship.

What makes one relationship more vulnerable than another?
So now that you have heard how an opportunity can open up the door for the actual affair to happen, let's backtrack a little bit and talk about the "why." Why can one person, given an opportunity to cheat, take it while another person doesn't?

When a couple comes into my office and infidelity has become an issue, I have a few questions that I want to get answers to right off the bat:

- What have you done to maintain the relationship?
- Do you go on dates together?
- How is your sex life?
- List the order of priority for the following three: your relationship, work, and family.
- How well do you deal with conflict?
- How is your communication, and do you communicate enough?
- Are your expectations for the relationship realistic?

What have you done to maintain the relationship?

When I ask a couple what they have done to maintain the relationship, rarely do I get an answer that shows me the couple is closely connected, making it a priority to spend time together, and communicating beyond the daily agenda.

When I say "maintain the relationship," this means doing things that keep both partners feeling that they are still important to each other, and creating opportunities to enjoy each other. Are you and your partner taking time to have fun? Do you continuing to learn about each other? Do you spend time together doing things and behaving in ways that remind you of why you even got together in the first place?

Some people would argue and say this is unrealistic—that you can't always act the way you did in the beginning of your relationship. Understandably, there is a change in the intensity and overall passion over time, but that's no excuse to give up working at the relationship altogether.

Relationship Rule: You MUST Continue Dating

I can't stress enough the importance of dating your partner. When I see the breakdown of a relationship, dating is rare or nonexistent. Sometimes, people even forget what a date *is*. I like to define "dating" as *intentionally setting aside time to be together while doing an enjoyable activity.*

Beyond the dating itself, I also suggest that you prepare for the date the way you did in the beginning of the relationship. This doesn't mean you have to go out wearing high heels and slinky clothes on every date (thought once in a while it might not hurt). It helps to be aware that men are visual, and their idea of "sexy and beautiful" rarely brings up an image of a woman in sweatpants and a sweatshirt. There is a reason men flock to the *Sports Illustrated* swimsuit edition, and it's not for the baseball batting averages. As much as your partner loves you for who you are and has feelings that go deeper than your physical appearance, looking good still matters.

I often suggest that a couple should try to date at least twice a month, if not every week. I cringe at excuses like "can't find the time" or "can't get a babysitter." These are solvable problems. Given the choice between making dating a priority in your relationship and losing that relationship to cheating, it's worth putting a little energy into making the date.

I also don't think a date is going to a movie, sitting side by side staring at the screen, and going home afterward. I'm not against movies—I think they're a great source of entertainment—but if this is the *only* way you can date your partner, your relationship may be in trouble. I am more of a fan of activities that create communication and shared experience.

When a relationship is already in trouble, it's not uncommon for a couple to avoid dating altogether, because they have all but forgotten how to enjoy each other's company.

Let's talk about sex . . .

Whether or not the couple in my office is dealing specifically with infidelity, I always ask the question, "How often are you having sex?" (And yes, it's implied that I mean "with each other.") The answers to this are always interesting to me. Usually, the wife thinks it's more often than the husband thinks. She might say they had sex four times last month, and the husband corrects her and says it was twice. In general, I find that the wife is satisfied with the frequency of sex, and the husband is not. I'm not going to throw out a number and say you need to have sex X times a week or month for your relationship to stay strong. There should be a conversation between partners discussing what their own expectations are for their sex life.

And frequency isn't the only issue to be addressed. There is also *quality*. It's important to define for your partner what a satisfying sex life means to you. A satisfying sex life is about so much more than frequency. Many people share that they could have sex less and still be happy if, when they did have sex, it was better. One partner might be frustrated because the other is not being adventurous enough. Sometimes one partner is so exhausted from the day that they just "check out" during sex. If you do not continually communicate with your partner about your needs and desires, before long, somebody's needs are sure to go unmet.

The subject of resuming sex after the affair is always tricky. My suggestion is that you try to focus less on what your partner did with his lover (if it was a sexual affair) and more on what he wants to do with you. Remember, resist the urge to get specific about the details of his sexual engagements with his lover. Try your best not to let feelings of insecurity, along with any imagined comparisons between yourself and their lover, consume your mind during sex. Yes, this is much easier said than done, but it can't go without saying.

Do you and your partner communicate?

Another question that provides much information about the couple is when I ask them to tell me about their communication. Here is one question I might ask: *"How long, on any given day, do you talk while completely engaged with your partner?"*

By "completely engaged," I mean that both of you are looking at each other while you are talking, with no competing distractions such as TV, newspaper, e-mail, and so on. More often than not, the answers reveal that the couple isn't spending much time in focused conversation together.

Priorities

Yes, life is busy. We work long hours, and our children have demands and needs that can't wait. But in a healthy relationship, there is an order of priority for the following three areas:

1. Marriage
2. Children
3. Work

Any change in this order can easily begin to create a problem in your relationship. It's also important that children see their parents carving out time for each other and making their relationship a priority. Not only is this great for the marriage, but it's also a good model for your children to integrate and take into their own marriage.

Setting priorities and making time to engage with your partner does not mean you are sitting and staring at each other for hours, scratching your head and trying to figure out what you can talk about. It really doesn't take much to get reconnected. You might ask your partner about the things that are important to him at this point in his life. Maybe you need to find out what really matters to him now. Follow up on concerns he is having about work, family, and friends. Your partner needs to know that you care and are willing to set aside the busyness of life to engage exclusively with him.

I have had couples admit to me that they don't even know what to ask or talk about. This is more common than you might think. In this situation, I give a homework assignment. I ask you to go on the Web and search the topic of "couple questionnaires" and print some out. You might find titles like "20 Questions to Ask on a First Date" or "30 Questions to Deepen Your Relationship with Your Partner." Anything that sounds remotely like that will work. As hokey as it might sound to you, these questionnaires can be the needed springboard for your discussions as you start getting to know each other again.

Conflict

How, as a couple, do you deal with conflict? Do you take turns talking and listening to each other and asking what you can do to solve a problem? Or do you and your partner just debate, trying to convince the other to agree with your point of view? When a relationship is in trouble, you'll find that communication is the first thing that breaks down, and conflict begins to increase. This is usually followed by an increase in arguing and yelling. Before long, the relationship is characterized by negative feelings. There is also the other extreme: an avoidance of conflict, where issues are just swept under the rug. The problem here is that the issues are still there. They haven't gone away and most likely will resurface.

As conflict starts to increase, the relationship starts to break down. The couple's previous sense of closeness, safety, and unity all but goes away. When conflict increases, one or both of you will be apprehensive about discussing issues you might deem "touchy," lest the discussion end in a fight. Choosing to avoid and not address these communication issues will quickly lead to somebody being dissatisfied in the relationship.

How Unspoken Expectations Can Contribute to an Affair

We have expectations for our relationship in a number of areas. If these expectations go undiscussed, discontent and disillusionment can come in and begin to characterize how you feel toward both your partner and the relationship.

Isolation and Loneliness

We are created to be relational beings. When you enter into a relationship, you have some expectation that you will spend significant time with your partner. You don't anticipate that loneliness and isolation will become defining factors of your relationship. When this expectation or need goes unmet, it may cause you to seek attention outside the relationship.

Regarding time spent with your partner, two types of relationship appear to be more vulnerable to an affair. One is the commuter relationship, where one partner works out of town and comes home intermittently—maybe on weekends, monthly, or even less frequently. The other is the relationship in which one partner serves in the military and is frequently away for long periods of time. If you find yourself in either of these types of relationship, you are wise to be especially vigilant. Note that I said "vigilant," not "suspicious." They are not the same thing.

Along with treating "commuter couples," I work close to a military community as well, so I often counsel couples who live the reality of a committed relationship defined by limited contact with their partner. From my observation, the tendency is for the individual who is left behind, managing the home, to become resentful toward the partner who is gone and *appears* to have no responsibilities outside work.

To make matters worse, inherent in this type of relationship is the dynamic of one partner at home handling the day-to-day, and the other traveling to exciting places, eating out in restaurants and having drinks with coworkers, and generally having to take care of no one but themselves. By all outward appearances, they are living the life of someone who is single. It's quite easy to see how this type of relationship can be the opportunity for an affair for *either* partner.

Another difficult reality for this type of relationship is the limited contact with your partner. Whether you communicate by e-mail, phone, or text or even try to Skype, these limited sorts of communication may not be enough time for you both to feel connected. The intimate communication between most partners is typically less about the big things and more about sharing small details of our lives. These details begin to get lost when you are only connecting electronically and for a very limited time each day. Conversations start to focus on the rundown of what's happening and the major things that need handling. You can see how easily connectedness might fall by the wayside. It's easy to see how this can lead to finding someone nearer by.

Hobbies and Work

Hobbies can be a problem when they are not kept in perspective. While it's healthy to have other interests and friendships outside work and home, if these interests get out of balance, the relationship can teeter on the brink of real trouble.

For example, your husband begins to golf more often, and there was no mutual agreement about how much time this would take away from the relationship, leaving you alone for longer than you find acceptable. The resultant loneliness can leave the door wide open for someone else to fill the gap. Resentment can kick in as you begin to feel less important than his hobby. I use the example of a male here, but women are just as guilty of letting their friends and interests take priority over time spent with their partner.

The same goes for the workaholic who gets up before dawn and comes home late at night because the job has become all-consuming. This is not to say that there won't be times when work is more demanding than usual and that a relationship can't accommodate that, but when you spend more time and energy focused on your work than on your relationship, you are sending a clear message. Remember the three priorities: the relationship is number 1, and work is number 3. Change the order consistently, and you court trouble.

Sometimes, work can be an escape from a relationship that has become negative and conflicted, but this is no solution to the problem. The anger that comes up when your partner puts his job above you can be quite intense—so intense that I have had some women describe their husband's work as "his mistress."

How Unspoken Expectations Might Play Out

Everyone goes into a relationship with their own ideas and expectations of how they expect to be treated by their partner. It's important to share with your partner your ideas about what you expect. Here's an extremely simplistic example to illustrate how unshared expectations can hurt a relationship:

Let's suppose that a woman expects her husband to give her flowers every week and to be taken away on vacation several times a year. This is how her dad treated her mother; therefore, in her mind, it's what a loving husband does. Meanwhile, her husband is unaware of this and does nothing for the first two years of the marriage: no flowers except on birthdays and Valentine's Day, and only one vacation a year. After the two years, his wife feels disappointed and resentful. In her mind, her husband's failure to treat her the way Dad treated Mom means he doesn't love or care for her. She then seeks solace in the arms of another man. A year later, she ends up feeling the same resentment toward her new lover as she did toward her husband. She is disappointed and feels neglected, all because she again failed to reveal her expectations. The affair could have been avoided had she taken the time to share her expectations about love and marriage with her husband from the beginning. (It still doesn't mean she would have gotten what she wanted, but they could at least have negotiated and been on same page).

I always tell my clients, "Your partner never got the manual telling him how he should love you—because no one ever wrote it. It's your job to teach him. It starts with each of you sharing your expectations of the other." I encourage you to have a conversation about your expectations with your partner. When expectations are clearly spelled out, it's much easier to avoid disappointment down the road.

"I love you, but I'm not in love with you."

This statement just makes my blood boil! Sorry about the emphatic wording, but seriously, this statement is so cliché, it should make you cringe, too. It's as if your partner somehow thinks it lessens the blow to hear "Don't worry, honey, I still do love you. I'm just not *in love* with you." That just makes it feel so much better, right?

Right. If someone says this to you, they are most likely ignorant of what love really looks like over the long haul. What they are really saying to you is this:

"I no longer get butterflies in my stomach when you touch me. When I see that you are the one calling, I don't drop everything to hear your voice. I am no longer consumed with thoughts of you, nor do I hang on every word you say, and wait on pins and needles for the next time we'll be together."

This is your brain on love.

This type of thinking shows a lack of understanding regarding the phases of love that all relationships go through. All relationships start out with the "in love" feeling. It's all passion and infatuation; feelings are intense and highly emotional; it's intoxicating stuff that actually creates chemical changes in your body. Your body is on a "natural high." In *The Science of Love: Understanding Love and Its Effects on Mind and Body*,[12] Anthony Walsh writes that your body has a release of dopamine, norepinephrine, and phenylethylamine—the "feel-good" chemicals of your brain. When you combine all this, you get what is called *romantic love*. As wonderful as it feels initially, these feelings will eventually decrease in intensity and begin to shift into feelings of *mature love*—that is, IF you don't leave the relationship before you get there.

In the transition from romantic love to mature love, there can be a sense of loss. The mistake is to attach "wrong meaning" to this transition. For example, believing in the illusion that true love carries with it a constant feeling of romance will tempt you to "jump ship" the moment you feel less passionate, less consistent positive feelings toward your partner—which are natural on the road to mature love. But if you can make your way to that mature love, you find a deeper bond that is secure and lasting. The commitment and connection over time bring a new level of intimacy and friendship.

The state of infatuation doesn't go on forever. If you or your partner don't understand this inevitable change, it's easy to buy into the lie and convince yourself, "I must be with the wrong person. The correct person for me is the one with whom I can always experience the intensity and passion of romantic love." Not so.

Blame Hollywood

Another way that unrealistic expectations about love affect relationships is when someone believes that their relationship is going to look like those in the movies. I've had people sit in my office and complain that the passion and excitement are gone after only two years of marriage. They come to the conclusion that the relationship is flawed, and attribute their disappointment to their partner.

As I begin to ask questions about their own ideas surrounding love and relationships, it isn't uncommon to hear them share an example from television or a movie. With so many marriages ending in divorce, and so many children growing up in single-parent homes, the big screen offers a fictitious example of love in the absence of a real one. To compare your relationship with those on the big screen can easily lead to the conclusion that your own relationship doesn't measure up or is in some way lacking. Reality looks boring when compared to Hollywood. But the thing to remember is that if the movies did mimic reality, they probably wouldn't be very entertaining.

A life of "Hollywood-style" relationships would most likely land you in a number of shallow yet highly sexual relationships that would eventually fall victim to cheating as you cast about to get the passion back each time the relationship started to lose its "sizzle"—not really the best plan. Understanding the source of your ideas about love is important when determining what went wrong in any relationship.

Other Ideas about Love

The model you see in your own family also forms your ideas about love. I encourage both you and your partner to discuss the influence your own families had on you and how it has affected your ideas about love and relationships. Whether it's the movies, family, or even past relationships, the dangers lie in letting any example of a relationship become the standard or definition of love.

Other Contributors to Infidelity

Life Transitions

Anytime there is a life transition, whether for good or for bad, it can put a strain on your relationship. It may be a wedding, the birth of a child, a death, buying a house, building a house, moving, or even taking a new job. While for some of us transitions can be exciting, for others they can be stressful. There's the unknown, along with the possible change in identity, lifestyle, and freedom.

A common example is the man who is both excited and scared about the birth of his child. He may feel an increased pressure to provide for the family in a way that he didn't before. Whether this pressure is real or not, this fear may set off a series of events that land him smack-dab in the middle of an affair. He may also seek comfort in the arms of another woman to soothe his feelings of neglect because his wife is so focused on the baby. When you go through these transitions, it's important to keep communication open and ongoing. So check in with each other and confirm that needs are being met.

Relationship Attacks from Friends

A relationship can become at risk when either partner chooses to surround themselves with people who are single, people who think cheating is acceptable, or people who have no respect for fidelity in a relationship. A man who finds himself hanging out with a bunch of single men (or men who are just plain horrible partners to their own girlfriends or wives) can begin to feel resentful and constricted by his committed relationship if his friends glorify the lack of expectations on them regarding their time, money, and leisure. Partners who choose to surround themselves with people who have wandering eyes or are consistently pointing out other attractive people can put any relationship at risk. I've had men tell me that they have friends who actually encourage them to cheat. Yes, sad but true.

Are some personalities more likely to cheat?

Two types of people seem more vulnerable than others to having affairs. These are people who have either *low self-esteem* or a *sex addiction.*

Those with low self-esteem seem to have such a void in their lives when it comes to needing affirmation, they seek out (maybe even unconsciously) the admiration of many. This person is not happy with the admiration of just one and is therefore always on the lookout for more. This can look like someone who has a narcissistic personality. They lack empathy and are completely self-absorbed with how *they* are feeling, at the cost of ruining their relationship with others. Not that they don't desire a committed relationship or don't love the person they're with. It's just that their internal drive for the affections and attention of others can override their ability to make good choices and stay committed.

The other type of person vulnerable to having affairs is someone with a sex addiction. I think people struggle to understand people with sexual addiction. This person does not necessarily cheat for any emotional reasons but, rather, gets a disconnected "high" from having sex with someone new. They don't really desire any relationship—just the release from having sex. Often, this intense need for sex is a result of feeling overwhelmed or anxious. They also tend to be impulsive in their behavior. Just as with any other addict, there are triggers to this behavior. The release they receive from sex is a coping mechanism that they use to deal with the pain caused by these triggers. They might even have a difficult time referring to these sexual encounters with others as "cheating," because this behavior is so impulsive and reactive. I've had clients tell me that they don't even remember much from their sexual encounters. They describe themselves as having been disconnected from "their real self" during these activities.

Going Forward

I hope it is clear to you that affairs happen for many, many reasons. There is not just one type of personality, factor, or situation that can predict who is going to have an affair. After reading all the different reasons that people choose to cheat, I hope you can find pieces of your relationship somewhere in those explanations.

I encourage you to take time to answer the questions at the end of the chapter to further explore what may have contributed to your partner's infidelity. This won't be easy to do, and I am proud of you for being willing to go to a place that will quite possibly be a very painful one.

In the next chapter, we will continue to explore your relationship and consider what factors you may have contributed to making the relationship vulnerable to infidelity.

— *Ask Yourself* —

1. Are any of the listed contributing factors to having affairs present in your partner's life (education, divorce, etc.)?

2. I mentioned that affairs can begin when a number of specific variables combine to form the "perfect storm," leading to the initial choice of having an affair. What variable do you think happened at just the right time to incite your partner in making the choice to cheat? Were you out of town? Was alcohol involved? Had you been fighting? Were you too trusting? Are there other reasons?

3. What area of your relationship might have been neglected at the time of the affair (for example, sex, communication, dating)?

4. Do you know what your partner's expectations are about love and relationships?

5. Was your relationship in the *romantic love* or *mature love* phase? How do you think that phase played a part in his choice to cheat?

— *Exercise* —

What are your ideas and expectations for love and relationships?

I want you to sit down with your partner, and each of you share where your ideas about love came from. I want you to ask these questions:

1. Do these sources provide a good model of love for you?
2. Are these models of love realistic?

After that, think about the expectations you have for each other in your relationship, and share them. Are there areas of your relationship that you both have neglected to be clear about, which may have made the relationship vulnerable to infidelity?

Chapter 7

So What Was
Your Part in All This?

Now comes the hard part: exploring your role in the infidelity. Up to this point, you have explored why affairs happen, who has them, and what types of relationship are most vulnerable to affairs. Now it's time to examine *your* contribution to the infidelity.

Before we move ahead, I hope you've taken the time to answer the questions and work through the exercises suggested in the earlier chapters. To be premature and jump right into this next topic can hurt more than help. This book is designed to guide you, step by step, by offering information and suggestions that can help you navigate the painful road of infidelity. Each chapter is built on the previous one, preparing you to address the relevant issues associated with each later phase.

Let's do a quick recap of the "action items" suggested up to this point:

1. You have done the information gathering and made the decision whether to confront your partner.
2. You have asked questions about the infidelity, and your partner has expressed remorse for his behavior. (If he hasn't, then we have a problem.)
3. If you and your partner are trying to restore the relationship, you have established new rules going forward.
4. You are *still* waiting to make a final decision about the relationship.

Unless you have addressed all these areas, exploring this next topic can be quite messy. If you're still reeling from the pain, or you question that your partner genuinely grasps what he's done to you, moving ahead can prove quite difficult. But if you feel that you are in a good and stable place, now it's time for you to sit back and listen to your partner's thoughts about the betrayal.

Envision the Conversation

I'm going to ask you once again to prepare mentally for this by envisioning the conversation. I want you to be ready to hear what he has to say. Picture the discussion. Imagine hearing some of the reasons you might expect him to give. This doesn't mean you're going to agree, but I want you to think about how you could respond. If you're not ready to do this, or if you find it just too difficult to listen to what part you may have played, you're going to be very defensive, and this will lead to an unproductive conversation. Until you can openly have this conversation, your relationship will remain stuck at the phase it's in now—or, worse, it might go backward.

If you avoid the opportunity to gain an understanding from your partner's point of view about what happened, it leaves you in a position of only *hoping* that you won't be cheated on again. Without understanding his side, you will explain away the affair by focusing only on what your partner did wrong. If you don't allow your partner the opportunity to share his point of view, your only hope of avoiding a future affair rests on his seeing the error of his ways. Ultimately, this choice leaves you powerless to prevent another affair, and I'm guessing that you do not want to be powerless. So go ahead, my dear. Brace yourself, and prepare for his explanation.

Asking the Hard Questions

So . . . do you believe that something you did may have contributed to the infidelity? I want you to think about that for a minute. Can you own a part of this? Is there anything that, just maybe, you could have done differently that would have made your partner feel differently about the relationship? Again, this doesn't mean you *made* him cheat. It doesn't mean he wouldn't have cheated if you had done things differently, but is there a possibility he would have made a different choice if things were different?

I am going to suggest that you approach your partner and ask him to share with you what part of the relationship he thinks might need improvement. Ask him what was going on at the time of the affair that made him so willing to betray you.

You may find out that he felt neglected. You may find out that you both were fighting too much. Maybe the suggestion he made about going to couples therapy should have been pursued rather than ignored. You might find that you're just not meeting his needs. You need to listen to your partner's specific reasons that he feels may have influenced the choice to have an affair. Then you should explore together how you can repair the relationship in light of this information.

I know, I just made that sound really easy. Piece of cake, right? Trust me, I know it isn't. I know that it will be very difficult for you to listen to your partner make any kind of excuse for his behavior. And because I know this, I am going to suggest a very specific task for you during this phase.

How to Listen without Losing It

I want you to decide, ahead of time, that you are not going to say a word. Yes, you read that correctly. You are not going to respond (at least not now) to your partner's reasoning. Your job is very similar to the one *he* had when you got to share how you felt about his betrayal. You will sit (as calmly as possible) and listen. This is going to take an extreme degree of self-control, I realize. I have no doubt you'll have to bite your tongue. And if that helps, fine—bite your tongue. Your job is to take it all in.

I encourage you to have a pen and paper and write down the main points of what your partner says. It may be hard later for you to remember everything he said, because your mind will be filled with questions, objections, and rebuttals as he speaks. Later, you will sit down by yourself and go over his reasons and give yourself time to digest what's been shared.

A good idea might be to talk over these reasons with someone who knows you well. They may be able to weigh in on some of what your partner shared, and let you know if they agree. Depending on how close you are to them, they may let you know if his observations also tend to ring true in their relationship with you. The hurt and anger you feel toward your partner may make it difficult to receive any criticism from him, so your friends and family are a safe place to seek an honest perspective on your behavior.

Once you've had time to go over the list, I want you to make another list. This one has all your questions and responses to what he shared. You will go back to your partner with this list and continue the conversation about how your relationship might need repair, and what parts you might be responsible for.

There is one exception . . .

You won't do this exercise if your partner is someone who cheats because he's a serial cheater. This is someone who will choose to cheat in every relationship, no matter how good or how bad it is. The serial cheater has a character flaw that prevents him from being committed to any one person. This person does not see this shortcoming, so in most cases, he will negate any attempt to have him realize that the betrayal was solely his choice. Aside from this type of person, it's safe to say that there are probably things you can do to make the relationship less vulnerable to an affair in the future.

Don't be afraid to ask for professional help.

At this point in the process of restoring the relationship, you may want to seek out some professional guidance. It can be helpful to have a third party available for these discussions, to help make sense of the meaning behind the reasons your partner listed and to give possible solutions. These conversations are not easy to have. You may still have difficulty accepting ownership for any of the reasons your partner lists. So don't hesitate to find someone who can mediate the conversation.

Now what do we do?

So what do the two of you need from each other going forward? Let's imagine he tells you that you were too busy with work. You justify that with the fact that he never paid attention to you. You now have identified two problems, and both are solvable. Ultimately, what it may boil down to is that you don't know how to make each other feel loved. I hear these words often: "It felt like you didn't love me anymore." This always brings me to the conversation about "love languages."

Do you know your "love language"?

There's a wonderful book out there by Gary Chapman, a marriage counselor. It's called *The 5 Love Languages*.[13] I highly recommend that you get a copy and go through it with your partner. The premise of the book is that we give our partners love in the way that we receive love. But to truly meet our partners' need for love, it must be in *their* love language. The book outlines five love languages that describe how most people give and receive love.

For example, one of the love languages is *gift giving*. So if you're the type of person who loves to receive gifts, guess what you're going to do? You are going to give a gift to the person you love! In your mind, this makes sense. It's a way to make them feel loved, because it makes *you* feel loved. It's going to make them feel greatly loved (so you think).

The problem with this occurs if your partner's love language is not gift giving but, say, *affection*. He feels love through hugs and kisses. All your gifts are a nice gesture, but it's not necessarily being translated as love. So imagine, year after year, you are giving gifts, and all the while your partner is just hoping you'll give them affection. Do you see how this can lead a person to feel neglected and unloved? To make matters worse, you might be getting lots of hugs and kisses from you partner as their way of loving you, but all the while, you're a little disappointed by never getting thoughtful gifts.

Chances are, neither of you is consciously aware of your own unique love language. These are the 5 languages Chapman describes:

1. acts of service: your partner's actions speak louder than words to you
2. physical touch: appropriate touch sends you the message that you are loved

3. receiving gifts: you feel most loved when you receive gifts

4. quality time: your partner's undivided attention is what makes you feel loved

5. words of affirmation: your partner uses words to make you feel loved

Once both you and your partner know how to express love in a way that is received, chances are that the relationship is going to be a lot stronger and, we can hope, not as vulnerable to a future affair.

Is there any hidden meaning?

I want you to begin to consider the *meaning* you have attached to the infidelity. What does it mean to you going forward? If you pay attention to how you talk to yourself about the betrayal, you might get some indication of its meaning for you. For example, you could be saying to yourself:

- "My partner cheated because I am not enough."
- "His infidelity implies that he is not the man I thought he was, and I should second-guess everything about him I ever believed to be true."
- "I should no longer trust my own judgment."
- "All men are cheaters."

This list could go on and on. You could be saying a lot of these things to yourself, and if you are not objective enough, these statements become truth to you. So you want to be very careful about the meaning you give to the infidelity, because the truth you derive from the meaning directly influences your "relationship rules."

Do you know your personal "relationship rules"?

Whether we are aware of it or not, we all operate by "relationship rules." As we experience life, we form these rules that shape the way we interact with one another. Often, we are clueless about the rules we make. For example, if you grew up in a home where you got the cold shoulder from your father anytime you disagreed with him, you might have a rule that says, *if you want to prevent someone from being negative toward you, then don't disagree.* Whether you notice it or not, these rules influence your behavior. Sometimes, the rules we make can prevent us from having healthy relationships.

> *Sarah, a beautiful, successful young woman, came to me over a troubled relationship. She was not the kind to have meaningless relationships. She shared that she hated dating and would make the effort only if she felt there could be a solid connection with that person. This had resulted in her having only two serious relationships. She was having trouble letting go of a terribly unhealthy relationship with her boyfriend. Once we began to explore her "relationship rules," we uncovered the belief that was making it difficult for her to leave the relationship. She told me, "You fall in love only once, so I have to make this work because I'll never fall in love again." Her rule was this: you get one chance at true love; all other relationships will be only*

a "lesser version." When I asked why she believed this, she really had no idea where it came from. It was just what she thought to be the truth about love. Once she really got that this was a rule she herself had invented, she had the power to change it. Ultimately, she made a new rule: true love can happen more than once. Identifying her maladaptive rule opened up unseen possibilities for her unhealthy relationship (such as leaving it in the dust, which she did). It's important to understand our own beliefs about love and relationship and how they influence our "relationship rules."

You have probably created your own set of "relationship rules" (functional or not), which you are completely unaware of. For example, if you have decided that your partner's betrayal means that all men cheat, you will create some version of the rule *never trust a man again*. The meaning you give to his betrayal will influence your "relationship rules" going forward.

Does his betrayal mean you should question your judgment of people? Perhaps, to protect yourself, you have made this rule: *be skeptical of everyone from now on.* How will your future relationships look if this is the rule you make? Rules also need to be challenged—especially those created out of pain.

What if you decide that the infidelity means you are not good enough and never will be? Imagine how you'll respond as a result of this thinking. Your confidence will be shattered, and, going forward, you will likely question your desirability to others.

Exercise: *What does the betrayal mean to you?*

I want you to fill in the blanks here:

- My partner cheated because _____.
- This means that _____.
- The way my life will now look different based on this reason is _____.

Now take a step back and really critique this. Does it sound right? If you are unsure, read it back to someone you trust. Let them help you assess whether you are being reasonable with the meaning you have attached to the infidelity.

Here is an unhealthy example of how someone might fill this out:

- My partner cheated because *I'm not good enough, and never have been good enough, to keep a man.*
- This means that *I will never be capable of having an exclusive and committed relationship*.
- The way my life will now look different based on this reason is that *I will accept my partner's cheating and be happy he hasn't left me altogether.*

Here is a healthy example of how someone might fill this out:

- My partner cheated because *we stopped making time for each other.*

- This means that *going forward, we need to make it a priority to go on dates and communicate in a meaningful way.*
- The way my life will now look different based on this reason is that *I will make it a priority to carve out time for my relationship with my partner before making plans with my friends.*

Remember to challenge the meaning you give to your partner's infidelity. Don't allow it to mean anything more than it should.

What's next?

At this point, you may be starting to ask the question: *When is it safe to make the decision whether to stay or go?* By now, I hope you have all the necessary information to make your decision. You know the role that each of you had in making the relationship vulnerable to infidelity. You know what it will take going forward if you decide to rebuild the relationship. You also have a better understanding of the elements necessary to "affair-proof" your relationship. Now is a good time to start considering the fate of the relationship.

This is the topic of chapter 8. You have arrived at the place where I encourage you to consider everything you have learned up to this point, and use it to guide your decision about the future of your relationship. If you need to, go back and review the questions you've answered at the end of each chapter, as well as the information you have gathered by doing the various exercises with your partner. And don't worry, just because chapter 8 is about "decisions" doesn't mean you should feel under any pressure to make one. This is just the next logical step in dealing with the affair. And just because it's the next logical step doesn't mean you have to take it now. You may not be ready to take that next step for a couple more months or even years. Let the upcoming information serve as a guide, not a timetable.

— Ask Yourself —

1. What is the meaning you have ascribed to his betrayal? How is it serving you? Is it helpful or hurtful to your ideas about love and relationships?

2. If you haven't asked your partner what he thinks you might have done to contribute to the affair, what is holding you back?

3. If you have already had that conversation, are you open to what he said? Is there anything preventing you from accepting his information as valid?

4. Do you think that what your partner sees as things you have done to contribute to his infidelity are things that can be changed? What must happen in your life to make those changes happen?

5. I want you to go back to the final exercise in this chapter and continue to fill it out for *all* the remaining reasons and meanings that you have assigned to his choice to cheat.

Chapter 8

Decisions and Forgiveness (Yes, It's Required)

Y ou made it!

If you have thoughtfully gone through all the previous chapters, my hope is that you now feel confident about pursuing the decision whether to stay or go. If you take a step back and observe your behavior with your partner, you may see some behaviors indicating that staying might be too difficult. Other behaviors may demonstrate that you are well on your way toward personal healing and toward integrating the meaning of the infidelity into your life. If this is the case, you can be hopeful for a positive future with your partner. Let's explore the signs to pay attention to as you head toward this decision.

Signs that Maybe It's Time to Go

Assuming that a significant time has passed since the revelation of the infidelity, I want you take a step back and consider some things:

- Do you feel just as hurt today as you did the day you found out about the betrayal?
- Are you still experiencing rage and anxiety regularly?
- Do you still feel a strong desire to require justice from your partner, and want him to continue making amends for what he did?

If these statements represent how you feel, there is always the chance that you have let the pain from the betrayal turn into resentment toward your partner and that it's just not going to go away. Even after all the steps you've taken toward restoring the relationship, you may find that things just aren't getting any easier. It may still be quite difficult to let your guard down, try to trust your partner, and relax in the relationship. If this is the case, the decision to move on from the relationship may seem the logical choice for you. Perhaps you have come to realize there is little chance of your being truly happy in this relationship that still lacks the element of trust.

Choosing to Stay for "the Other Reasons"

You may be one of those individuals who don't make a decision based on their feelings—a good way to make decisions, actually, since feelings can be deceiving. You have considered all the other important factors that make leaving the relationship a complicated decision (children, money, values about marriage and divorce, and so on) and choose to stay *despite* knowing that you can't trust your partner.

If this is your decision, I want you to envision how this relationship is going to look in the future. Making the decision to stay while still not trusting your partner doesn't mean you have permission to hang on to the anger and resentment. By deciding to stay, you understand that you've made this choice based on thoughtful consideration of all the options. If you are confident that staying in the relationship is necessary for you at this time, I want you also to choose to be at peace with this decision.

The priorities you set in life will more than likely point you to the answer for the "stay or go" question. If a happy home environment is your priority and you are in a relationship with a lot of yelling and belittling, you may come to the realization that even though there is some "good"—such as financial security and having an intact family—it is no longer worth the emotional toll. The toxic yelling and carping creates a negative home environment, thus challenging your priority. So you make the decision to go.

If your priority is to avoid a broken home, then the "cost" yelling and a negative home environment will justify the "good (in this case, the intact home). Now, please know that I am not encouraging anyone to stay in a negative home environment. I'm just pointing out the reality that some people will make this choice. I work with plenty of clients who are ashamed or embarrassed to admit that they are going to stay in a "less-than-perfect" relationship. Gambling, pornography, debt, affairs—these are all real scenarios that people deal with. As terrible as they are, many choose to stay in relationships where these things affect them daily.

There is no right or wrong answer to the question "Do I stay, or do I go?" What puts one person on the brink of an emotional meltdown can be quite bearable, perhaps even comfortable, for another. Just as each of us comes into a relationship with family history and baggage that shape our desires and hopes for each relationship, what may break us is equally variable. The right answer is YOUR answer. This answer becomes the "why" to whether you leave or stay.

Know your why.

Once you know your "why," you can put the "stay or go" question to rest. Here's an example:

> *Joanna, a hardworking woman who had been married for eleven years, was frustrated and ready (again) to throw in the towel on her marriage. Her spouse had repeated the mistake of making a big financial decision without consulting her (even though he had promised after the last time). She felt that all-too-familiar pain*

from the last spending spree. As she considered how to respond to her husband, I suggested she revisit the reasons why she had made the decision to stay with him after the last spending spree. She told me, "As angry and let down as I felt, I chose to stay because my priority, both now and then, is an intact marriage over financial peace."

This is her "why." You may have to go through a similar process when your decision to stay for "other reasons" feels challenged. I can assure you that you will remind yourself more than once why you chose to stay in this less-than-ideal relationship.

Finally, once you make your decision, do not reconsider it unless . . .

- your priorities change or
- your partner's behavior changes.

Having that familiar, draining debate in your head every time you are irritated by your partner will rob you of your joy and peace. So save yourself the grief.

What will this look like for you?

You will choose not to feed the anger and resentment. You will not punish your partner for the betrayal. Nobody is holding a gun to your head while you make this decision to stay, so you need to take responsibility for that choice, knowing it won't always be easy for you. As we discussed earlier, don't fall prey to "what if?" thinking. This is a sure formula for depression. Don't go around and around and keep analyzing the decision *after you've made it*. The time for questions is *before* you make the decision, not after. Once you have made a decision, you then live life the best you can, *pursuing* peace while living out this difficult decision to stay.

Don't let this choice to stay (which may mean you have compromised your ideals about a relationship) steal your joy. If the specifics of your life that influenced your choice to stay should change, perhaps your decision will also change. But until then, do your best to forge ahead and find a new way of relating positively to your partner, in spite of what has happened. Don't let the infidelity overshadow every part of your life. You have permission still to pursue happiness!

He still doesn't know what he wants.

Maybe you've noticed that your partner has gone through the motions of saying he's sorry, but you don't see any follow-through on any of the decisions and rules you've made to help restore the relationship. You can't help but notice that all his attempts seem halfhearted at best. This can make it terribly difficult to trust that he is invested in a relationship with you. What's worse, if nothing changes, you may fall prey to constantly living in a state of paranoia, wondering whether he really wants to be with you.

Take a good, hard look at how invested your partner seems to be in enriching and rebuilding the relationship. Once a relationship has taken a hit like this, both of you should be in overdrive when it comes to caring for each other in the relationship. If your partner seems to be "reconciled" to being with you, that doesn't bode well for a happy future together. In fact, he may just be putting off the inevitable without even being aware.

There is always the chance that your partner doesn't want to be in the relationship, but the guilt over what he has done leads him to stay. It's his own emotional battle over what has happened that keeps him in the relationship. I've seen it happen where the betrayer wants to do the "right thing." His choice to stay is a moral, or ethical, one. He feels the need to make amends for his betrayal by staying loyal to his hurt partner. Doesn't sound very romantic, does it?

If your partner verbalizes that he wants to keep the relationship, yet still seems detached in every other way, perhaps it's time for a discussion about what the affair means to him. You get to take all the wisdom you gained by learning what the infidelity meant to you in the last chapter, and help him apply it now. Use the same exercise in chapter 7 with him. See if you can't draw out what is going on in his mind and how he is making sense of it all. (Who knows? You might have fun being the one in the therapist's chair.)

If you can make it comfortable for him to explore the meaning of the betrayal along with his own feelings about the relationship, together you can discuss what might be the best choice for both of you going forward. Again I reiterate, you do not want to be with anyone who doesn't truly want to be with you. Both of you deserve better than that!

You don't want the relationship (but thought you did).

Maybe you really don't know what you want, even though you thought you did. Some people go immediately into rescue mode at the revelation of infidelity. When you are in rescue mode, it appears you have made the decision to stay in the relationship. At the news of the affair, you dived impulsively into saving the relationship. Unfortunately, this knee-jerk reaction kept you from examining the relationship in any constructive way. You neglected to consider whether you were even happy in the relationship. When you are in rescue mode, your only focus is to remain in the relationship with your partner—at all costs. Your number one goal is to get things back to "normal" as fast as you can. In rescue mode, you are driven by fear of the unknown. For you, the fear of a life without your partner, even if you were miserable together, is stronger than your desire to have a healthy and stable relationship.

What can happen after you eventually get things "back to normal" is that you finally start to consider how healthy or unhealthy your relationship was. Now, after fighting so hard to get the relationship back, you might find you don't even want it.

Decisions Based on Fear

Choosing a relationship out of fear is not a good reason to stay. You might be influenced by fear if you think:

- I'm too old.
- I'm too fat.

- I can't make it on my own.
- I'm not pretty enough.
- If he doesn't want me, nobody will.
- I'm damaged goods.
- Everybody cheats, anyway.

And the list goes on.

Are these the reasons you're going to stay? Are you going to let yourself believe that nobody else will want you or that it's too late to start over? Or buy into the belief that you can't trust again, so why bother? Don't let those unfounded fears keep you in a bad relationship. To live out life in a relationship that you have "settled" for is not the best suggestion for a fulfilling and peaceful life. This will have a negative effect on you emotionally. It welcomes in all kinds of insecurities, which have far-reaching effects on many other areas of your life. I want you to decide that you are going to take better care of yourself than that. Be protective of your own identity, and don't allow the infidelity to chip away at your confidence, because this will only limit you in the future.

Forgiveness (Oh, no, not that!)

If you choose to go forward with a relationship, whether with your partner or with someone new, at some point you need to decide to make a fresh start. If you decide to leave your current relationship, you must intend to leave it completely behind— emotional baggage and all. Don't make the next person pay for what your betrayer did.

I encourage you to take some time and make sure you truly have healed from what happened, *before* you start over with someone new. Be careful not to get into a relationship too quickly. If you feel the need to make your new partner earn your trust all the time, or find that you are constantly checking up on him, you may not be ready to move ahead just yet.

If you do not take the needed time to process what has happened and to understand why your partner cheated, you are quite likely going to be suspicious of the next person you choose to be in a relationship with. It just wouldn't be fair—to him or you. Don't make your next partner pay for the wrong of your last relationship. Take the time and try to understand why the infidelity happened.

Whether or not you decide to stay with your partner, you won't be able to escape the issue of forgiveness. This is the sticking point for many. The road toward forgiveness seems like a scary passage indeed. But if you've been betrayed, the need for forgiveness will show itself at some point in the healing process.

A Definition of Forgiveness

Whenever the subject of forgiveness comes up in therapy, it's not uncommon to hear the fearful and protective response: "No, I can't possibly forgive what he did!"

Forgiveness has gotten a bad rap. I think this is because there are so many definitions out there about what, exactly, forgiveness is. Some think it just means to forget, move on, and not stay angry. Others say it is something that must be earned. I often discuss forgiveness in the light of how you personally apply it in your life. In other words, how will you behave toward your partner when you have forgiven him? Concepts can be difficult to understand, but *behaviors that result* from a concept seem easier to grasp.

I use this definition of forgiveness: "Forgiveness *is* a choice to release someone from owing you anything. It *is not* forgetting, excusing, or condoning. It *is* letting go of the anger and resentment.

Let's look at some common hindrances to forgiveness after infidelity.

Hindrances to Forgiveness

Forgiveness is making the decision to stop expecting something, beyond the apology, from the betrayer. When you don't forgive, you are constantly expecting him to make up for the pain he has caused you. You might not even know what it is that you want—all you know is that you haven't gotten it.

I've worked with couples when no amount of remorse was ever going to satisfy the person who was betrayed. This mind-set can have you unknowingly take on an attitude of *entitlement*—feeling you deserve to be given something. This attitude conveys to your partner that he must earn the right to be in the relationship with you. This, my dear, is not forgiveness.

Are you feeling entitled? If you're wondering, stop and ask yourself this question: *How will I know when I have reached the point where I feel that my partner has done enough to earn my forgiveness?*

You probably realize that it will be almost impossible to know when that day comes. It's unrealistic to think that all of a sudden, you'll wake up and say, "Now I can forgive my partner. He has done enough."

When forgiveness is seen as something to be earned, this means that new "rules of engagement" are in place. The betrayer takes on the identity of the *groveler,* and the betrayed becomes the *all-powerful judge.* (Right—not the stuff romances are made of.) In this new dynamic lies an unseen danger, which can lead to the cycle of infidelity repeating itself. Here is how this dynamic played out for one couple I saw:

> *Before Dan turned to a lover to meet his needs, he felt all but ignored by his high-powered executive wife, who seemed to have it all under control: the kids, the house, and the finances. After revelation of his affair, Sandra wanted to keep the marriage. Although they were still "together," Dan couldn't miss Sandra's arrogant attitude toward him, which served as an unspoken reminder that he was to be grateful for his wife's decision against a divorce and behave in ways that showed it ("kiss her butt," in other words). Sandra's anger and humiliation created a coldness in the relationship, which brought up the same feelings of loneliness that had led Dan to have his affair in the first place. Now more than ever it seemed that the only way to get the love, attention, and tenderness he so desired was to get it outside the relationship. Dan was committed to not cheating again, so he was left with the option of either staying in misery as he continued to wear the scarlet letter, or moving on from his marriage.*

To hang on to the pain of the betrayal and withhold forgiveness from your partner can be a poison that kills your relationship far more surely than the actual infidelity.

Forgiveness is a gift.

Don't operate out of the belief that your partner can completely "earn" your forgiveness. At some point, you will need to risk vulnerability and meet him halfway, extending grace to him by choosing to forgive. By definition, grace is something that is not earned or deserved. Your choice to forgive will be a gift of grace.

If you choose to stay in the relationship, you will daily choose forgiveness (yes, you read that correctly: *daily*). You will no longer remind your partner how he hurt you. There is often a hesitancy to forgive, because we tend to equate forgiving with forgetting. We fear that if our pain is forgotten, it will no longer be acknowledged. This is why it's so critical to feel that your partner has *acknowledged*, deeply and honestly, what you have been through. If he doesn't acknowledge the experience you went through, you will feel compelled to acknowledge it for him. If you still feel the urge to remind him often about his transgression, pursuing forgiveness won't be easy.

This is the reason I stress the importance of your partner saying "I'm sorry" to you over and over again in those earlier phases of addressing the infidelity. Innately, you know that if they can grasp how hurt you are, they are less likely to repeat the offense.

Moving to the opposite extreme, I would question someone who agrees to forgive immediately without first seeking to have their partner understand their experience. To move too quickly into forgiveness is to disregard your own need for validation, and this would make me wonder whether you were acknowledging your feelings in the first place.

And please, don't assume that forgiveness means that you have *no expectations* about your partner's future behavior. You can forgive him while still remaining cautious toward him. To display warranted hesitation in trusting your partner does NOT mean you haven't forgiven him.

Understanding is not a requirement for forgiveness.

I want to caution you: don't wait around for the day when you finally feel that your partner *completely understands* the pain he has caused you. It's not going to happen. You need to let go of that idea or expectation. Don't delay forgiving your partner because you feel that his understanding is a prerequisite to your forgiveness. Instead, I want you to consider:

1. Has your partner listened to you, over and over again, as you have expressed your pain to him?
2. Has your partner responded to your hurt by showing genuine remorse for his actions?
3. Has he taken the necessary steps toward rebuilding trust in the relationship?

These are the behaviors that should encourage you to extend forgiveness to him.

The decision to move toward forgiveness actually needs to come earlier rather than later. When you make the decision to pursue restoring the relationship, you are deciding that you *will* work toward forgiveness.

Forgiveness is necessary not only if you choose to stay. It's just as important if you choose to go.

Even if you decide to leave this relationship, seeking forgiveness benefits you.

Forgiveness helps release the hurt and anger, so it is less likely to taint your next relationship. If you don't forgive, you are in danger of carrying around the pain of the betrayal and making everyone else pay for your partner's infidelity. And if you think you're too self-aware to let that happen, good luck with that. It's subtle; more often than not, you won't even know you're doing it. I've seen people who have been cheated on and are so stuck in the pain from the betrayal that years later, they are still alone—not by choice, but because their choice not to forgive has kept them from trusting anyone.

This same person, unable to forgive, may develop a pattern of many short-lived relationships. If you choose not to forgive, it's quite possible that every time you get close to someone, you will find a reason to leave, because the last time you loved somebody that much, they hurt you. Worse yet, you may buy into the belief that infidelity is inevitable—that all people cheat.

Choosing to forgive early on—whether you stay or go—will lead to the healthiest relationships in your future. And it also results in a healthier you. The person who gets hurt the most by not allowing forgiveness is you. When you don't forgive somebody, you actually stay in bondage to them. Every day, you are connected to them emotionally through your bitterness and resentment. *You* want to be the one in charge of your emotions.

Don't give that power over to them and what they did to you. Forgiveness cuts off that attachment. When you forgive, you release both the betrayer and yourself. You move from being a victim to becoming a survivor.

Forgiveness signifies that you have survived this journey through infidelity.

Making It Official

I'm a big proponent of rituals. I encourage my clients to create or participate in rituals so they have a point, marked in time, that they can look back on and refer to. For example, in the final session, I might ask a couple to write letters or vows and read them to each other. They may formally make a commitment to the future of the relationship and each other or even have a ceremony to renew their vows. Each of them may ask for the final time, "Will you forgive me?" and hear from the other, "Yes, I forgive you." I encourage you to explore with your partner anything that signifies your commitment to this renewed relationship. Let that significant event be the start of your new beginning.

If you have chosen to leave your relationship, I still encourage you to do a ritual. I want you to look back on a point in time that marks when you also chose to move past the infidelity and into your new life.

Infidelity is now a closed chapter in the unfolding story of your life. With or without your partner, you are moving into a new chapter. The chapter that ends with forgiveness gives way to a chapter that finds you hopeful and strong, and knowledgeable about the vulnerabilities of relationships and the individuals who form them. Your transformation from who you were to who you are now has been long and trying, but the end result is well worth the effort!

The End of the Journey:

Stepping Out Together in the
New Relationship You Both Have Created

I feel as though I am saying good-bye after a long journey with a dear friend. I sit here and imagine you, who have allowed me to walk alongside you as you go through this process of decision making and of rebuilding your relationship and your life.

I can picture you stronger from this. You accepted the challenges that came at you, and chose to learn more about yourself and your partner. I admire you for pushing aside your pride and making some difficult changes to your relationship and your life. I honor you for going forward with no guarantees of how things would turn out, having only the hope that there must be something better on the other side to hang on to.

It's always hard to say, "I am stronger because of this." Inherent in that statement is the idea that you are *thankful* for what happened. I know that you wouldn't wish what you have gone through on anyone. If there were a better way to arrive at a better and stronger relationship, you would have taken it.

But the reality is, you both *are* stronger because of it. If you have survived infidelity, there is probably very little that could now tear the two of you apart. You have chosen to go forward in life with your partner—a second time. You had every right to leave, but here you are. In spite of it all, you chose him—again. Most likely, you are more aware today of why you are choosing your partner than you were the first time around. Sometimes, we neglect to appreciate someone, until we almost lose them.

The depth of intimacy between two people that results from the trial by fire of surviving infidelity can be understood only by those who have gone through it. You have been given the gift of a deeper, stronger, more fulfilling, and, ultimately, better relationship because of what you both have experienced. But for the way it had to come about, you would be the envy of others.

As you go forward together, continue. Keep on building a life that allows infidelity to take its place as a pivotal event in your relationship—but not the *defining* moment. I hope you will decide in your heart to relegate the pain of the betrayal to only a moment in the history of your relationship—a moment to be overshadowed by the joy, stability, and depth of intimacy that is, and will be, the overarching theme of your life together.

About the Author

Laurel Wiers is a licensed marriage and family therapist who has been in private practice for over fourteen years. She is the owner and director of Lighthouse Counseling in Groton, Connecticut, and founder of www. therapydiva.com, an online site offering resources and products for individuals wanting help with struggling relationships. She received her master's degree from East Carolina University while doing her internship at Duke Medical Center as a counselor in the Cancer Patient Support Center. She has served as an instructor at both East Carolina University in North Carolina and Mitchell College in Connecticut. She has been an expert contributor for publications in the *Chicago Tribune*, gURL.com, careerbliss.

com, naturalnews.com, and *Military Life* magazine, to name a few. She has been interviewed by both authors and radio personalities on the subject of infidelity, appearing most recently on the *Michael Dresser Show, Engage-Woman 911,* and *Gfem Talk Show* in Atlanta, Georgia.

Laurel and her husband, Eric, have three young children and make their home in Ledyard, Connecticut.

Endnotes

1   Peggy Vaughan, overview report of "Survey on Extramarital Affairs," 1999, www.dearpeggycom/results. html.

2   Steven D. Solomon and Lorie J. Teagno, "Frequently Asked Questions about Infidelity," 2013, www. divorcemag.com/articles/Infidelity/Infidelityfaqs.html.

3   Todd K. Shackelford and David M. Buss, "Cues to Infidelity," *Personality and Social Psychology Bulletin* 23, no. 10 (1997): 1034-45.

4   Peggy Vaughan, *The Monogamy Myth: A Personal Handbook for Recovering from Affairs* (New York: New Market Press, 1998).

5   D. C. Atkins, N. S. Jacobson, and D. H. Baucom, "Understanding Infidelity: Correlates in a National

Random Sample," *Journal of Family Psychology*, 15 (2001): 735-49; Denise Previti and Paul Amato, "Is Infidelity a Cause or Consequence of Poor Marital Quality?" *Journal of Social and Personal Relationships* 21 (2): 217-30.

6   M. W. Wiederman, "Extramarital Sex: Prevalence and Correlates in a National Survey," *Journal of Sex Research* 34 (2): 167-74.

7   Atkins, Jacobson, and Baucom, "Understanding Infidelity," 735-49.

8   Ibid.

9   Judith Treas and Deirdre Giesen, "Sexual Infidelity among Married and Cohabiting Americans," *Journal of Marriage and Family* 62 (2000): 48-60.

10   Atkins, Jacobson, and Baucom, "Understanding Infidelity, 735-49.

11   Shirley Glass, "Consumer Update: Infidelity," American Association of Marriage and Family Therapy, August 22, 2013, www.aamft.org/families/consumer_updates/infidelity.asp.

12   Anthony Walsh, *The Science of Love: Understanding Love and Its Effects on Mind and Body* (Buffalo, NY: Prometheus, 1991).

13   Gary Chapman, *The 5 Love Languages* (Chicago: Northfield, 2010).